EDUCATING AMERICA ///

Lessons Learned in the Nation's Corporations

JACK E. BOWSHER

WILEY

JOHN WILEY & SONS, INC.

New York / Chichester / Brisbane / Toronto / Singapore

Publisher: Stephen A. Kippur
Editor: David Sobel
Managing Editor: Frank Grazioli
Editing, Design, and Production: G&H SOHO, Ltd.

The opinions expressed in this book are the author's and do not necessarily represent the opinions of IBM Corporation, or any professional education association with whom the author is affiliated.

This publication is designed to provide accurate and authoritative information in regard to the subject matter covered. It is sold with the understanding that the publisher is not engaged in rendering legal, accounting, or other professional service. If legal advice or other expert assistance is required, the services of a competent professional person should be sought. FROM A DECLARATION OF PRINCIPLES JOINTLY ADOPTED BY A COMMITTEE OF THE AMERICAN BAR ASSOCIATION AND A COMMITTEE OF PUBLISHERS.

Library of Congress Cataloging-in-Publication Data

Bowsher, Jack E.
    Educating America: lessons learned in the nation's corporations /
Jack E. Bowsher.
       p.   cm.
    Bibliography: p.
    ISBN 0–471–60066–0
    1. Education—United States—Aims and objectives.   2. Industry and education—United States.   3. Employees, Training of—United States—Case studies.   4. School improvement programs—United States.
I. Title.
LA217.B69   1989
370'.973—dc19

88-39747
CIP

Printed in the United States of America

    90 10 9 8 7 6 5 4 3 2

This book is dedicated to

CHARMIAN

My partner on this project
and my partner in life.

Permissions

Grateful acknowledgment is made to the following for permission to use material appearing on the pages listed below:

Pages 16, 17: Reprinted with permission from *Let's Put America Back To Work* by Senator Paul Simon, © 1987, Bonus Books, Chicago.

Page 22: *A Nation Prepared: Teachers for the 21st Century* by Dr. Marc S. Tucker, © May, 1986, National Center for Education and the Economy.

Pages 27, 28: "Are We Spending Too Much on Education?" by Peter Brimelow. Adapted by permission of *Forbes* magazine, December 29, 1986, © Forbes, Inc., 1986.

Pages 34, 35: Reprinted with permission from *Saving the New Corporation*, published by the American Society for Teaching and Development, © 1986.

Page 44: Reprinted with permission from "Corporate Education and Training" by Thomas J. Chmura, © 1987, SRI International.

Pages 54, 55: Reprinted with permission from "General Motors Philosophy of Training," © 1985, General Motors Corporation.

Pages 157, 158, 173: Reprinted with permission from "Investing in Our Children," Research and Policy Committee of the Committee for Economic Development, © 1985.

Page 159: Reprinted with permission from "Attitudes Toward Primary and Secondary Education Systems" by Kenneth L. Otto, © 1986, *The Business Roundtable*.

Pages 165, 166, 173: Reprinted from *Winning the Brain Race: A Bold Plan to Make Our Schools Competitive* (ICS Press), © 1988 by David T. Kearns and Denis P. Doyle.

Pages 193, 194: "The Untouchables" by Peter Brimelow. Adapted by permission of *Forbes* magazine, November 30, 1987, © Forbes, Inc., 1987.

Page 197: Reprinted with permission from *College: The Undergraduate Experience in America,* by Ernest Boyer, © 1986, Carnegie Foundation.

Page 202: Reprinted by permission from *Higher Learning* by Derek Bok, Harvard University Press, © 1986.

Page 222: Reprinted with permission from "Confronting the New Reality," © April 1987, Council on Competitiveness.

Page 226: Reprinted with permission from "How to Smarten Up the Schools," by Myron Magnet, © February, 1988, *Fortune* magazine.

Acknowledgments

This book, as is true of most books, has a long history. Over the years, a number of people and experiences have influenced my ideas and convictions. While I am entirely responsible for writing the book, I would like to acknowledge some individuals who have made significant contributions to my knowledge and career in education.

First, I owe sincere thanks to Ursula Fairbairn, the IBM director responsible for the healthy functioning of educational programs throughout the company's worldwide operation, and to Lew Gray, IBM's retired vice president of education. They supported the implementation of all the major elements for restructuring employee education that are discussed in this book.

Second, I would be remiss if I did not acknowledge IBM's chief executive officer, John Akers, and the management committee, which made important contributions to the process of education by reviewing and approving the restructuring of employee education at IBM during the past five years. Tom Liptak, the retired vice president of organization, was another member of the executive team who gave his personal leadership to this strategic project.

Third, I owe special thanks to Walt Burdick, the IBM vice president of personnel, and to Ed Krieg, who five years ago gave me the opportunity to coordinate education programs throughout the company. I also want to thank George Barry, another IBM personnel executive, who was my senior partner during the reorganization study that resulted in the centralization of education as a line organization.

All the directors and managers of education with whom I have worked during the past 20 years have also contributed to many of the concepts outlined in this book. And I owe a special thank-you to the hundreds of people who have worked for me in the 12 management positions in education that I have been fortunate enough to hold during this time period. Regrettably, space limitations prevent me from listing each individual and his or her contributions.

The five people who were asked to read an early draft of the manuscript and who provided important feedback to me obviously deserve to be named: John Splavec, John Rosenheim, George Haskell, Carla Paonessa, and Dick Johnson. One person in particular made this book substantially more readable than it would otherwise have been: Dr. Herbert R. Miller, who introduced me to instructional design methods in 1973. He has been my partner on many education projects, and he contributed a number of important improvements to this book. And my son, Robert Bowsher, with his creative writing abilities, provided many helpful points of editing.

A sincere note of thanks is due to Andy Neilly, the president of John Wiley & Sons, who took the time to read my initial outline and passed it on to one of his editors, David Sobel, who was my consultant on this endeavor.

And, finally, I owe some special words of appreciation to my mother and father, Ella and Matthew Bowsher, who believed so strongly in the value of education and who sacrificed so much so that my brother and I could have the benefit of a college education.

Contents

Introduction

Many Americans who graduated from the public school system before 1965 feel they received a very adequate education. After all, our education prepared us to hold almost any position in U.S. society. I, personally, am a graduate of the Chicago public schools and the University of Illinois. Today, my fellow classmates are architects, judges, bankers, lawyers, engineers, school administrators, teachers, ministers, professors, doctors, business executives, government officials, and social workers. No other country has logged such an impressive record in educating the masses. The education system provided us, the children of working-class families, with the opportunity to move into some of the most responsible and exciting positions in our society. We are all grateful.

We all assumed that the fact that only 25 percent of our classmates did well and enjoyed school was a normal part of the education process. The next quartile did not enjoy school as much as the top quartile, but they struggled through and seemed, by graduation, to have survived the system that constantly reminded them that they were second best. And we thought it was not unusual for 50 percent of the class simply to drag through 12 years of schooling. These students really hated school because they were frequently told in various ways that they were the bottom half, the lazy ones, the failures. As I remember, we did not have many dropouts, but I believe many more would have dropped out if they had thought they could. School was an unpleasant experience for them, and the judgment "you will never be successful" probably scarred them for life.

In those days, few people suggested a major overhaul of the education system. Education was education. You followed the rules and the traditional process of education if you wanted good grades—and those of us in the top quartile wanted good grades.

Today, there is much discussion regarding the involvement of parents with schoolteachers. As I remember, most of us did not want our parents coming to school because that would have meant that we were not getting good grades or that we were in some type of trouble. We were all relieved when "parents night" was over. Parents never talked about changing the school system. They simply said, "Work hard and obey your teachers."

All this has changed. During the 1980s a new and exciting interest in the subject of education has arisen. Almost every politician is speaking about the need to improve education. Many business executives have added their voices to the discussion, and the voices of those who have served as Secretary of Education under the Reagan administration have brought the discussion an unprecedented level of national attention.

Terrel Bell, the first Secretary of Education under President Ronald Reagan, released the widely acclaimed report from the National Commission on Excellence in Education, *A Nation at Risk,* which boldly stated that education in the United States was not working. Former President Reagan's position changed dramatically as he went from wanting to close the Department of Education to being an advocate of improving the American education system. His second Secretary of Education, William Bennett, was even more vocal about the need to restructure our nation's schools.

Everyone seems to be in agreement that the education system must be restructured for any real breakthroughs to occur in the quality of education. The group pressing for improvements in our educational processes includes the president of the Carnegie Foundation for the Advancement of Teaching, deans of graduate schools of education, presidents of universities, superintendents of schools, and business executives, including many chief executive officers of leading corporations. Business organizations such as the Chamber of Commerce, the Business Roundtable, the National Alliance of Business, the Committee for Economic Development, the Conference Board, and so on, are issuing reports and speaking out on the need to restructure our education system. Teachers' unions and professional education associations are also deeply involved in the push to improve our school systems. And governors have sponsored one commission after another focusing on the need to improve performance in state school systems. It is rare, nowadays, to hear anyone saying that schools do not need to make fundamental changes.

All these studies, task forces, and commissions, mean that thousands of people are now at work on the issue of how to restructure schools. More and more people are looking for breakthrough solutions to the large and complex problems that have been identified. The publicity that the many reports have generated has alerted millions of Americans to the failure of education in our country. They are eager to know the answers to the fundamental problems faced by our schools. They expect more than an attendance-based system—they want to see performance.

Unfortunately, no consensus exists on what the breakthrough solutions might be. Most study groups eventually publish huge reports containing long lists of problems but that devote only a few final pages to some generalities called "solutions," which in general would require massive increases in the cost of education.

In 1986, when I, as director of education for the IBM Corporation, was struggling to come to grips with problems of employee education, I started to read the reports issued by various commissions and to attend meetings on the problems of education. These experiences eventually led me to write this book.

A little of my background may serve to illustrate why I feel qualified to author such a document. I began work as an accountant in 1953 after graduating from the University of Illinois with an accounting degree. Including my work as an accountant in the U.S. Army as well as my eight months with a large steel company, I practiced that profession for about two years. I decided to further my financial career by earning an MBA from the University of Chicago with a major in finance. Then my career took a major change in direction.

IBM offered me a position in its marketing organization in 1956, at the beginning of the "computer age." Taking the job turned out to be one of the great decisions of my life. First, I participated in an outstanding training program. IBM's program gave its employees so much confidence and self-esteem that we had the courage to call on the senior executives of the world's largest corporations to show them how to restructure the flow of information in their complex organizations. This was a long way from selling beer mugs in the fraternity house a few years earlier!

For many years, IBM's marketing organization helped to revolutionize the business world with new information systems. We guided our accounts from unit-record punched card equipment through batch accounting systems to database–data communication systems. It was a rare experience to be in your twenties and thirties with so much responsibility to create and implement change. My own account was Sears, Roebuck and Co. I will always be grateful to its executives for allowing me to help them restructure their basic information systems.

In 1968, I was asked to join the marketing education department of IBM, after having managed large-account marketing for two years. Again, this turned out to be one of the great decisions in my life, because over the next 20 years I was to have the opportunity to work in every major area of employee education, including teaching, managing groups of teachers, managing education centers, and developing courses. Initially I developed courses in my spare time, with no training on how to create high quality educational programs, but, later with the assistance of instructional designers, media experts, and professional writers, I designed an array of courses for advanced technology classrooms, for satellite classrooms, for self-study, for computer-based training, and for videodiscs and personal computers that were of the highest quality.

In late 1983, with a background in finance, marketing, personnel, and education, I was presented with the challenge by IBM's vice president of personnel to coordinate all employee education within IBM, whose program includes 7,000 full-time educators and support staff who together conduct several million days of education each year. On any given day, more than 18,000 IBM employees attend some educational event, so the work of coordinating IBM's employee education is similar to managing a state university or a city school system. During the past five years, education inside IBM has been substantially restructured in spite of its already having had a national reputation as providing one of the finest education systems in the country.

Why have I told you so much about my background and experience? Well, the question may naturally arise among many readers of this book, "Why is a book that describes a revolution in education being written by a businessperson rather than an educator?" As I sit in meetings with noted educators and superintendents of large school systems, I realize that most of them have never had the experience of developing a curriculum of courses or of developing courses that use the advanced delivery systems that are available today. They have not been immersed in the process of education at a level that would enable them to look for those areas where fundamental changes in the learning process can be made. This experience has always been viewed as belonging to education research. Unfortunately, education research has played a minor role in the reform movement. The education leaders have been involved in budgets, personnel issues, policies, and other general management subjects. Many are unable to discuss instructional design techniques because they have never been trained in nor involved with that subject.

Business executives and government leaders usually have even less knowledge about the process of education. Attending meetings with these people, I feel as if I am among people who want to restructure the automobile industry, but whose only experience with automobiles has been that of driving. They have never participated in the design, engineering, manufacturing, or distribution areas of the business. Educators, politicians, and executives have, therefore, been looking for a quick fix to the problems. Though tutoring, mentoring, "adopt-a-school" programs, career days, and so on, have all been tried and all have probably made some small increase in the quality of education, it is doubtful that such programs, or the more sweeping reforms involved in instituting a longer school-day, merit pay systems, well-defined career ladders, new systems of organization, smaller school size, new school buildings, or even more pay for teachers could solve all the problems that the task forces have identified.

On the fifth anniversary of the "Nation At Risk" report, Secretary of Education Bennett presented President Reagan with a report showing that all 50 states had adopted reform laws, 40 had raised graduation requirements, and 15 had completely overhauled their education systems. But, he said, "the toughest phase of reform is still ahead." Later, Bennett stated that we are *still* a nation at risk: He, along with many other educators, feels that the current reforms have helped the top quartile or at most the top two quartiles of students. The bottom half of the class is still in trouble. The dropout rate decreased only two percentage points—from 30.5 percent to 28.5 percent—between 1982 and 1987. The process of education is still not working even after billions of dollars have been spent. In fact, the SAT scores dropped in 1988 for the first time since 1980, and this marked the third straight year without a gain.

A Carnegie Foundation report, entitled, "An Imperiled Generation," has said,

America must confront, with urgency, the crisis in urban schools. Bold aggressive action is needed now to avoid leaving a huge and growing segment of the nation's youth civically unprepared and economically unempowered. This nation must see the urban school crisis for what it is: a major failure of social policy, a piecemeal approach to a problem that requires a unified response.

Business, government, and education want to restructure schools, but they just do not have a vision or a plan for implementing the changes that will bring about a substantial improvement in the process of learning. This is why I decided to write this book. After restructuring education at IBM, I strongly believe that there is a process of education that will apply to all areas of education—not just employee education. The objective of this book is to describe how education can be restructured to achieve the following results:

- The vast majority of students would do well and would like attending school.
- Almost everyone would master the lessons, by which I mean the equivalent of their receiving a grade of A or B. We would continue to be able to recognize outstanding performers, but *all* students would feel successful at learning.
- The label "bottom half of the class" would disappear, as many discipline problems would be eliminated due to better performance.
- The successful method of learning would build self-esteem and good citizenship.
- Twice as much learning would take place. Yes, double the number of lessons would be successfully taught in science, geography, history, and other basic subjects.
- The American workforce would be given the chance to be once more the most competitive workforce in the world.
- Prison populations and their huge costs could start to decline, because formerly illiterate inmates could now obtain jobs that would utilize their new knowledge and skills.
- Welfare costs could decline by billions of dollars, because the millions of "unemployables" could obtain jobs and become productive workers, paying taxes rather than receiving handouts.
- The number of dropouts could decline from almost 30 percent to as low as a few percent.
- School administrators would earn salaries akin to those of business executives, because outstanding performers would be in demand as each city would try to improve its school system.
- Teachers would receive well-paid professional salaries, because their performance would be rewarded according to new measurements of quality.
- Everyone could learn—rich, poor, black, white, hispanic, urban, rural, young, and old.

This is a vision that business executives, government officials, and educators should possess when they meet to talk about restructuring education—*not* moving SAT scores up or the dropout rate down a few percentage points. Basic restructuring is possible in the 1990s. No new technology is required; no major breakthroughs in research are necessary; and no huge amount of money is required to achieve the needed results.

Speaking of costs, let's look at where we are today and where we are going. Here are the nationwide costs for the four major areas of education:

Annual Cost

$185 Billion:	K–12
125 Billion:	Higher Education
40 Billion:	Employee Education
25 Billion:	Continuing Adult Education
$375 Billion:	Total in 1988

At the rate education is growing, the total cost will reach more than $400 billion by 1990. By the mid 1990s, it could be $500 billion—that is, half a trillion dollars! To keep that number in perspective, note that the United States will spend $290 billion on defense in 1988. If we are able to reduce our defense expenditure in the 1990s, as many predict, our education budget could well be twice that of defense before the decade is over. All this money for a process of education that is not working.

Why do I keep using these three words—the *process of education?* Let me explain by using an analogy from computer manufacturing. Imagine you're in charge of a large organization that manufactures computers. Suppose nearly 30 percent of the computers never make it off the production line; another 20 percent are labeled failures—not usable—and will have to be warehoused, at substantial cost, for 40 years; the second quartile are acceptable, but not great. You are proud only of the top quartile from the production run. What would you do?

Your immediate reaction would undoubtedly be to take a look at the process of manufacturing. You would never suggest running daily production a few hours longer or paying the managers and workers more money with the hope they might make better computers. You would not waste time discussing merit pay. Nor would you immediately want to decentralize the decision-making when the output is so bad. Your entire focus would be on the *process.* Likewise, it is time to study the *process of education* before billions more dollars are added to the cost of education. This book represents an attempt to motivate the leaders of government, business, and education to shift their time, knowledge, creativity, and resources away from defining the problems toward finding breakthrough solutions.

Some of us have been working on improving the process of education for a number of years. Now is the time to surface with these solutions and to share them with the leaders capable of creating major changes in our education systems. Education can be fixed. With the knowledge of how people learn and the technology available today, education systems can be built that will ensure that the vast majority of students will learn.

This book is sure to be criticized by some traditional educators. They will say that it lacks education research. Some will even deride it because the writing style is simple rather than academic. Others will claim that business is totally different from education. Some will fall back on the old, tired argument that there is a big difference between education and job training. But those who cannot accept change in the education systems of today must accept dropout rates of 20 or 30 percent, millions of unemployable high school graduates, and the United States' international reputation of being almost last in performance while being first in expense. No one wants to continue with this vision of the American education system.

A great parallel can be drawn between the growth of our education expenses and the tax structure of our country. Years ago, local property taxes paid for local public school systems. The 1- or 2-percent state sales tax paid for the state universities. In the past 25 years, the states have increased their sales taxes and added income taxes to become the major source of funds for public schools and state universities. Many people are predicting that in the 1990s the federal government will try to pass a consumption tax, sometimes called value-added tax, or VAT, that will cost the taxpayers billions of dollars, all in the name of improving schools. Why not? After all, a majority of states have implemented lotteries in the name of improving schools.

Again, one has to ask the question, "Are there any breakthroughs in the process of education that we can begin employing now?" This book will show where these breakthroughs have been achieved. It will also provide a case-study of how to restructure education. The final five chapters will discuss how the lessons learned in one area of education can be applied to the other areas of education. There is a process of education that is applicable across many areas of education. To achieve this breakthrough we must energize millions of people. People must believe in a new vision for education. A partnership of government, business, and education must agree on the vision and together adopt a plan to create massive change. The revolution in education in the 1990s has already started within employee education.

I predict that the federal government will soon fund the restructuring of education within inner-city schools. If the lessons of this book are applied, the new vision described earlier will be achieved in our most challenging school systems, which will in turn lead suburban schools to implement new courses and new personal tutoring systems. Continuing adult education will be the next area to restructure itself. Eventually, colleges and universities will evolve from their present condition of unstructured education to one that is highly structured, but this will probably not happen until the next century.

As I write this book, I am making another major decision in my life—early retirement from the IBM Corporation. I should point out that no other IBM employee was involved in the writing of this book. It does not represent the opinion of the IBM Corporation nor of any professional education association of which I am a member or officer. It is a personal endeavor to communicate my own convictions on how to restructure education.

Many people have come to meetings and briefings at IBM, asking

- Why do your executives support education?
- How do you justify your budgets?
- How did you raise the quality of education?
- How do you control the cost of education?
- How do you measure education?
- How do you manage education?

It has taken me a lifetime to learn and practice the lessons contained in this book. The joy of sharing them with the people who work on a day-to-day basis to improve our educational institutions has been the motivation for writing this book.

This book will provide a bridge of information between government agencies, schools of education, leading educators, school systems, and organizations with large employee-education programs. We need the best thinking of all educators to achieve major breakthroughs in education. This book challenges each reader to say

- There is a systematic method of improving the quality of education.
- There are ways to reduce the cost of education.
- The real challenge to education is leadership and the management of change.
- There are no excuses for having substandard education systems anywhere in our country.

This book will surely create debate within the education community. Its success will not be measured by the number of copies sold. The true measurement will be found in its ability to accelerate the restructuring of schools in the United States. As public education systems improve, the standard of living will also improve. The improved education system will ultimately become a worldwide process that can benefit millions. It is truly a noble cause.

PART 1///

THE NEED FOR RESTRUCTURING EDUCATION

1 ///

Two Major Problems Create the Need

Few human endeavors involve as many people as education. Learning, both formal and informal, takes place in every country, city, town, and village and in every language. Recent reports show that formal education in the United States costs about $375 billion each year. In fact, in the United States education provides jobs for 7 percent of the workforce and consumes 7 percent of the gross national product, and it is estimated that 40 percent of Americans are enrolled as students in some type of education or training program each year.

A majority of people do not see the education process as very complex. The average person believes that education involves little more than a teacher standing up in a classroom and telling the students what he or she knows about a subject. The students take notes and are periodically tested on whether they have memorized the key lessons.

Actually, the process of education is much more challenging than this. Among its elements are the following:

- A clear definition must be drawn up ahead of time concerning what knowledge and skills the students are to learn.
- Course materials and instruction methods must be carefully constructed to motivate the students.
- Lessons must be clear and must be presented in a way that enables students to learn them.
- Students should be involved during the course through activities

such as exercises, and they should be tested at the end of the education event to determine whether they have learned the key lessons and are able to demonstrate the skills that the training has been designed to provide.

SIGNS OF TROUBLE

Obviously, this process is a great challenge to implement, because many schools are receiving very low marks, even after five years of effort to improve their performance. Here are some of the problems commonly cited:

- Most students do not like school; many even hate to go to school. Further, they are "turned off" by school at an early age.
- Teachers are unhappy. They not only feel underpaid but also believe that students and parents do not appreciate their efforts. Worse yet, teachers are often in conflict with their school administrations and local school boards. Strikes and threatened strikes have been common in past years.
- Many university professors try to avoid teaching undergraduates. They want to write, to do research, and to work as consultants. When they must teach, they much prefer to teach graduate students.
- Taxpayers are rebelling in many communities. They see increases in education budgets in spite of decreasing enrollments in many communities. They also feel that today's schools have declined in quality compared to when they attended.
- School board members and university trustees are caught in the middle. They have the unhappy students and teachers on one side and the unhappy taxpayers on the other.
- Most parents are displeased with the quality of education, the lack of discipline in schools, and the performance of their sons and daughters. They are terrified by the ever-rising costs of a college education.
- Business executives become concerned about education once they find out how much money is being spent on employee training. Corporations' growing education budgets are evidence that high school and university graduates are poorly prepared to enter the workforce.

- Politicians talk more and more about the crisis in the classroom and claim that education will be one of their top priorities if they are elected.

TWO MAJOR ISSUES IN EDUCATION

Reading about all the issues surrounding our troubled school systems and listening to "the experts" discuss the various challenges now facing educational institutions brings you to the conclusion that two major problems afflict the education process:

1. The cost of education is rising faster than the rate of inflation, and most proposed solutions for improving education require huge sums of money.
2. The quality of education has declined at a time when people need to know more in order to take their place in the workforce.

These two problems give rise to major issues that must be confronted if we are to address the concerns listed in the introductory section of this chapter. How do we raise the quality of education at the same time that we try to contain its escalating costs?

CONSEQUENCES OF NOT ADDRESSING THESE PROBLEMS

Overall, our educational system is in a state of crisis, and the resulting problems are having a profound impact on our country. To date, we have not addressed these issues successfully. Here are some of the consequences that result from our not finding solutions to the major problems:

- Crime is increasing, and the costs of the legal and penal systems are rising.
- A growing number of people cannot qualify for productive jobs, increasing the cost of welfare programs.
- The rising toll of economic competition from other countries, where products of equal or higher quality can often be manufactured at lower cost. Many of our employees do not have the knowledge or skills to be competitive.

Crime is one of the major problems facing the United States. Reports indicate that one out of four American households is affected by crime each year. That is certainly a shocking figure, and your response is likely to be, "Can that be true?" until you hear the statistics. The nightly news on TV sounds like a police report. Almost every state in the nation is constructing additional correctional facilities, which makes you think that crime is one of the major growth industries in the United States!

Ineffective school systems certainly contribute to the growth of crime. If a high school graduate (or dropout) cannot read or write, has bad work habits, and does not get along with people, then he or she will often turn to crime to find money for survival. Of course, the school systems should not take all the blame, but they are part of the problem.

When a citizen has acquired a police and prison record and cannot read or write, that person has little chance of holding a full-time productive job. This unfortunate reality is one reason why most people released from prison will eventually return. Education in most penitentiaries fails to train inmates for jobs. Too often, prisoners leave jail as they entered, without being able to read or write.

Another major problem in the United States is unemployment. There are two aspects to the issue of employability: a young person's ability to get a job once he or she has left school and that person's ability to stay employable as technologies change. The nation was pleased when the unemployment rate dropped to 7.2 percent late in 1986, but we should not lose sight of the fact that between the Great Depression and 1980 there were only two years (1975 and 1976) when the unemployment rate was that high. Senator Daniel P. Moynihan of New York has accurately noted, "Rates of unemployment that were thought intolerable in the early 1960s are thought unattainable in the 1980s."

Senator Paul Simon of Illinois, in his book *Let's Put America Back to Work,* presents some very interesting insights:

- Under the leadership of President Harry Truman, Congress passed the Full Employment Act of 1946, making a commitment in words to provide employment opportunities to all Americans. Truman was worried about one million unemployed people. Over forty years later, with ten million people unemployed, the hope and promise of that act remain unfulfilled.
- When we talk about roughly six or seven percent unemployment, that does not count two to three million Americans who are working part-time. If an American works one hour a week, that person is counted as

employed. The 6 or 7 percent count what the Bureau of Labor Statistics calls "the discouraged worker," the person who has simply given up, who is no longer looking for a job. The Bureau estimates that more than a million "discouraged workers" exist in this country.

- No one knows precisely. Ten million unemployed may understate joblessness slightly, but it is probably close to accurate. Ten million people is almost twice the population of Switzerland. If Switzerland suddenly would have no employment, the U.S. Government would galvanize our resources to help the Swiss people. Lions Clubs and Women's Clubs and churches and synagogues would volunteer help. As they should! But when more than twice the employable population of Switzerland is unemployed within our borders, the United States has yet to make it a matter of national concern.
- Three realities should cause a change in our national employment policy: First, the demand for unskilled labor is declining. That trend will not change. Second, the pool of unskilled labor is growing. Third, we are not going to let people starve.

All these facts lead to the conclusion that a national demand will arise for major training programs to elevate the "unemployable" labor force to a level at which its members will be able to obtain and hold productive jobs.

In 1987, the National Alliance of Business issued a report that sums up the reasons why the demand for job training will increase:

- Workers will change jobs five to six times during their normal work lives.
- Twenty to forty percent of those dislocated are functionally illiterate.
- Over one-fifth of all dislocated workers lack a high school education.
- A total of 1.5 million workers are permanently displaced each year and will require assistance to reenter the work force.
- By the year 2000, an estimated 5 to 15 million manufacturing jobs will require different skills from today's jobs, while an equal number of service jobs will become obsolete.

Our country should be proud that in the late 1980s our unemployment has fallen to the low, 5 percent range, but a major concern remains. Our country will continue to be split into two worlds of citizens: The first group will be educated, will have productive jobs, and will lead a life of individual choice. The second group will depend on government programs for food, health, housing, energy, and transportation. Members of this group will be unable to hold jobs, even when work is available, because of their lack of education and basic work habits. As the second group expands and the first group (or tax-payers) declines, resentment over having to pay taxes for the masses who do not work will grow.

It should also be noted that drug use is high in many areas where there is a high rate of joblessness. Alcoholism is even higher than drug use among the unemployed. As a result, the federal budget suffers. President Ronald Reagen used the figure that one million unemployed people cost the federal government $28 billion. Others have used the even larger figure of $35 billion. These figures include federal expenditures for food stamps, welfare, unemployment compensation, Medicaid, and a host of other costs, including the loss of tax revenue. Many people believe that investment in education could help reduce these figures and the federal deficit. Unfortunately, most people also believe that putting additional resources into current educational systems would not put people back to work—and they may be right. Previous job training programs like the Comprehensive Employment and Training Act (CETA) have cost billions of dollars with minimal results. Major changes may be necessary in our educational systems before people are willing to invest in them.

A third major problem in the United States involves our increasing inability to compete in a worldwide marketplace. We need to improve our ability to respond quickly to changing situations and to have the flexibility to change direction in the scene of global competition.

President Reagan appointed John A. Young, chief executive officer of Hewlett-Packard, one of this country's major corporations, to head a task force to study America's industrial competitiveness. That group bluntly told the American people, "Our ability to compete in world markets is eroding. Growth in U.S. productivity lags far behind that of our foreign competitors. Real hourly compensation of our work force is no longer improving. U.S. leadership in world trade is declining."

In 1983, the National Commission on Excellence in Education stated in its report, *A Nation at Risk,* "Our once unchallenged preem-inence in commerce, industry, science, and technological innovation is being challenged by competition throughout the world." To meet that challenge, the report called for major changes in education. Sub-stantial modifications are required, the report maintains, because of facts such as these:

- The United States continues to be the only country in which a student can earn a doctorate without ever taking a foreign language course.
- Only 8 percent of our universities require foreign languages for ad-

mission and only 5 percent of our college graduates are fluent in any foreign language.

- A United Nations study of 30,000 ten and fourteen year olds in nine countries demonstrated that American students ranked next to last in their comprehension of foreign cultures.
- Geography is more than knowing the names of capitals and mountain ranges; it is the study of people, their environment, and their resources. Americans lag far behind other industrial nations in geography education.

In the 1950s, a worker in Virginia competed with workers in South Carolina or South Dakota. In the 1980s, the competition comes from Asia, South America, or Africa. Economist Lester Thurow states,

America's fundamental problems remain unresolved. America is every day becoming less competitive in world markets. If the present trends continue, America's standard of living will fall relative to those of the world's new industrial leaders, and it will become simply another country like Egypt, Greece, Italy, Portugal, Spain, and England that once led the world economically but no longer does.

We cannot improve our competitiveness by lowering wages. Instead, what we can and must do is give our workers outstanding equipment and the best education possible.

In *Let's Put America Back to Work*, Senator Simon raises the following question:

"Why has Japan made such tremendous strides, moving from an income that was 5 percent of the average American's income in 1950, to 67 percent in 1984?" Japan, a nation the size of California, and half our population, has few natural resources. Yet Japan has surpassed most nations in economic growth through developing ideas and human potential. The Japanese have announced a goal of having the world's highest per capita income by the year 2000, and few contest the possibility of that happening.

A recent Department of Education report, *Japanese Education Today,* that compared the Japanese and American education systems states,

Japanese society is education-minded to an extraordinary degree. Parent-teacher relationships are strong plus the ties between school and business are close. Student motivation is high. The Japanese school week is 5½ days long, and vacations are shorter. Japanese classes are larger, but more orderly than those in America. Students are better behaved and more attentive, and as a result they spend about one-third more time during a typical class period engaged in learning.

THE NEED FOR BREAKTHROUGH SOLUTIONS

We may hope that pessimistic outlooks like those expressed by Thurow, above, contain a flaw. They ignore the possibility that major changes in our education systems could revitalize the workforce. Nothing restricts the future as much as our present failure to use American human resources more fully. We must find breakthroughs in the productivity of our workers. One of those breakthroughs must come within the education systems.

When business executives, government officials, and educators search for breakthroughs in our education system they often focus on the following issues.

1. Can we find a breakthrough in teacher salaries?

In 1987, the National Education Association reported that the average salary for the nation's 2.3 million public school teachers is $29,573. We can assume that this figure will continue to increase at about the same rate, which is higher than the rate of inflation. In fact, over a ten-year period, teachers' salaries have almost doubled. For example, in 1986, when consumer prices rose less than 2 percent, the average teacher received a 6.8 percent pay raise. The jump in schoolteacher salaries in the 1980s has been sparked by education reform programs and by the general feeling that teachers are underpaid. (Schoolteachers currently receive salaries lower than those of most other college graduates.) But for this trend of doubling teachers' incomes every ten years to continue, there must be a breakthrough in the quality of education or, as it is sometimes stated, the amount of learning must show a dramatic increase. Teachers have much to gain from a restructured education system that corrects dropout problems and improves student performance. Major increases in teachers' wages without corresponding changes in the performance of the education system will require billions of dollars in new local, state, and federal taxes, and taxpayers are unlikely to support such increases through the 1990s unless they see an education process that works. The lessons in this book can be a start toward achieving an education system that is successful.

2. Can we find a breakthrough in job satisfaction?

On January 5, 1987, NBC News telecast a "White Paper" program called "To Be a Teacher" in which network anchor Tom Brokaw profiled the plight of America's schoolteachers. The program brought back many memories for those of us who watched.

According to the program, the typical teacher teaches five classes a day as well as having an additional supervisory duty, such as study hall or cafeteria duty, for the sixth period. The experienced teachers, who teach advanced students, appeared to enjoy their jobs, but new teachers are typically assigned average or below-average students, and they were portrayed as struggling in their jobs. One remarked, "Our task is to trick the students into thinking they are having fun and hope to teach them a few facts in between the fun situations." Most of the students, though, didn't see how they would ever use the lessons being taught. Most were "turned off," and some even said they hated school. Students were critical of their teachers' dress, mannerisms, and capabilities. Yes, the students were evaluating the teachers, and the teachers were getting low marks.

The teachers felt they spent too much time on discipline, administrative tasks, and nonteaching assignments. Morale appears to be very low. Teachers do not feel they are supported by school administrators or by parents. They claim that teaching is a thankless job. Many have second jobs, and the positions at which they moonlight often take on more meaning than teaching. Of course, this other work usually means they have less time to grade papers and plan lessons.

Both the students and the teachers seem to express a resigned attitude: we are here because the law says there must be schools, teachers, and students. On average, each student is in school for 15,000 hours from first grade through high school graduation. Some students made this sound like 15,000 hours at hard labor!

The most depressing scene in the documentary portrayed a young woman doing her practice teaching in preparation to be certified as a teacher. She had neither the confidence nor the skills to motivate and teach the students. She poured her heart out to the students, saying in exasperation, "We both have to be here. Let's make the best of it."

Various studies tell us that job satisfaction among teachers appears to be very low and if that, anything, it is getting lower. While the school environment has often changed, the job of teaching has not changed much over the years, and few see it changing in the future. Fortunately, some teachers do thoroughly enjoy their jobs, but most teachers are in schools where no fundamental changes have occurred in the education process. Restructuring schools is absolutely necessary if the working conditions of teachers are to improve.

3. Can we find breakthroughs in attracting outstanding young people to the teaching profession, and can we provide them with new methods of teaching?

The Carnegie Forum on Education commissioned a task force on teaching as a profession, *A Nation Prepared: Teachers for the 21st Century,* which published its findings in May, 1986. The report makes the following points:

- After years of teacher surplus, in 1985, jobs and job seekers were roughly in balance.
- For at least the next ten years, however, there will be more jobs than applicants.
- Simply because of impending retirements, many school districts face a situation in which half of their teachers may have to be replaced in the next three or four years.
- The children of the children of the "baby boom" are now entering school. Thus, we can anticipate a steep increase in the annual rate new teachers must be hired from 115,000 new teachers in 1981 to 215,000 in 1992 by conservative estimate. Between 1986 and 1992, 1.3 million new teachers will be hired.
- Although the proportion of entering college freshmen declaring an interest in a teaching career increased during the last three years from a low of 4.7 percent to 6.2 percent, this followed a fourteen year period during which such interest plummeted by 80 percent.
- Many of the most accomplished teachers who are now in our schools have told interviewers that they would not choose teaching if they were beginning their careers anew.
- Many more professional opportunities are open to able young women and minorities. College educated women who until recently had a choice of becoming a secretary, nurse or teacher can now, like the members of minority groups, choose for the first time from a great array of attractive possibilities.
- The proportion of minority students is also increasing. At the same time, the proportion of minority teachers is declining.

The evidence is strong that there will be a shortage of teachers during the next ten to fifteen years. More teaching positions will probably be filled by noncertified teachers, which, unless the education system is greatly improved, is the only practical solution.

There is no strong evidence that the colleges of education that train future teachers will offer dramatic new teaching methods that will cause a breakthrough in education. New teachers simply are not going to be better trained than are existing teachers, and we can only hope they will be as good as some of the teachers who will retire in the 1990s.

If we are to attract "the best and the brightest" to the teaching profession, students must be able to see a new vision for education that clearly shows that the restructured schools will improve the process of education.

4. Can we find a breakthrough for increased student involvement?

A survey of a better-than-average school in Connecticut revealed that two-thirds of all students devote less than two hours a day to homework, while they spend more than two hours daily in sports and extracurricular activities. In fact, the survey reported that 68 percent of students spend 15 minutes or less on homework per night per course. Fewer students are using study halls to study, with only 33 percent using their free periods to do homework. Seventy-six percent of all students typically spend less than an hour preparing for a test. It should also be noted that as the shortage of workers grows for fast-food outlets, retail stores, and other basic jobs, there will be greater monetary incentives to work after school rather than to study.

The consensus appears to be that American students spend less time on homework than do students in Japan and Europe. The amount of study time is decreasing and will probably continue to go down unless the process of education changes to provide more individualized learning, challenging students through the use of a personal tutoring system. A restructured school system must allow for individual learning time rather than expect success from old-fashioned homework assignments.

5. Can we find a breakthrough in maintaining student interest in school and learning?

Some school administrators and teachers feel that today's teachers, as a group, are as dedicated as were teachers in the "good old days". They feel that society has changed, not teachers. Students do not have the support they once had to be successful in school. For example,

- More and more young people come from homes that are not stable, let alone secure or serene. During recent years, the proportion of students from broken homes has risen from 10 percent to more than 50 percent. Many adolescents now deal with that instability and with the kinds of issues that once confronted only adults.
- It is hard to believe the statistics on drug abuse and alcohol. However, we must assume that many students have parents with

problems related to substance abuse, which in turn undoubtedly reduce the emphasis on schoolwork.

- The most pervasive distraction in the higher grades is the allure of sex. The media show that sex is full of pleasure and promise. Teenagers have lots of free time and, because their parents work, are unsupervised during the day. Teenage pregnancy is the major reason why girls drop out of school.
- The media present young people with the message that everything must be fun and entertaining. Classes are boring compared to television. Homework isn't fun either, and it must compete with titillating "soaps" and cable-TV movies.
- Finally, in the two-income family, both parents work so much that they have little time to take interest in their children's schoolwork as much as they want to.

One thing is certain: We cannot wait for all the problems of society to be fixed before we begin to restructure the school system. One of the goals of the restructured schools must be to create a process of education that makes school work interesting and motivational. Students must feel challenged in a positive manner and must find some practical value in the majority of their lessons. This may require a massive effort in the development of new course materials.

6. Can we find a breakthrough in reducing the number of dropouts?

A study by Alexander W. Astin, *Minorities in American Higher Education*, states that 83 percent of white children complete high school. Only 72 percent of black students complete high school. Even more shocking is that only 55 percent of Chicanos, Puerto Ricans, and American Indians complete high school. This adds up to millions of students who drop out. Almost every state has developed some type of dropout prevention program. In 1986, a Senate subcommittee recommended spending $50 million to help reduce the number of high school dropouts, who are estimated to cost society billions annually in lost taxes, unemployment, welfare, and crime.

Committees and study groups throughout the country are trying to find a solution to the rising number of school dropouts. Many dropouts are students who speak Spanish or another foreign language at home and so have never obtained a functional grasp of English in their elementary schools. By the time these students reach high school they are sitting in classrooms listening to lectures in a language they don't fully understand. Other students, who are native speakers of English, have been moved along by the system over the years in spite of their poor academic performance. Now they, too, are sitting in classrooms where they cannot handle the materials being taught.

The Ford Foundation recently gave $1.1 million to 21 cities to find out why the number of dropouts has grown so large and to devise strategies for countering the problem. Despite this and other efforts, however, the dropout problem has only slightly improved. Unfortunately, at the present time there appear to be no real solutions to the dropout situation. The overall education system needs to be improved, rather than relying on dropout prevention programs in high school to lower the rate of students quitting school. We can no longer have 50 percent of students disliking school. Fundamental changes are necessary and possible.

7. Can we find a breakthrough in addressing the literacy crisis?

One wonders how students cannot read and write after spending thousands of hours in school. On September 3, 1986, ABC aired a documentary, hosted by Peter Jennings, entitled "At a Loss for Words: Illiterate in America." Jennings reported that 13 percent of all adult Americans are illiterate. That's 20 million men and women who cannot read or write well enough to cope with the simplest communications of everyday life—20 million adults at a loss for words!

Beyond the 20 million illiterates, at least 20 million more Americans are marginally literate. They read at or below the eighth-grade level, recognizing but not really understanding basic words. The world we live in runs on words and numbers, but a study found that 13 percent of adults could not properly address an envelope. The same study found that, given a store receipt, 28 percent could not make the proper change. Functional illiteracy is now jeopardizing the American economy.

Jim Cates, director of the Literacy Project at the University of Texas, has said, "It's my firm conviction that the United States faces no greater threat to our national security, or to our continued dominant position in the world community, than having such a tremendous percentage of our population functionally illiterate."

In the past, the requirement for many jobs was physical strength— brawn, not brains. But jobs relying on manual labor are disappearing. This country is changing fast. As we move toward high technology and become an information-based society, we increase our demands for literacy. Over the next four years, 80 percent of all new jobs will require more than a high-school education. Later in this book, you will find that there are programs that exist today that will be able to achieve a breakthrough in literacy.

8. Can we find a breakthrough in the use of technology?

Computers have been talked about in educational institutions for over 30 years. Early educational uses of computers demonstrated that students could learn with computer-assisted instruction. The cost of computer networks in the 1960s—networks that included mainframes, storage devices, and terminals—were far beyond the economic reach of most schools. Yet, less expensive personal computers have been in use in school systems for almost ten years with mixed results. With quantity and education discounts, a fully functional personal computer system can cost less than $1,000. A system with much less function may cost as little as $500 or under.

So far, computers do not appear to provide a breakthrough in the quality of education. Here are some of the reasons:

- Many teachers do not have the training to properly use the systems in the classroom. Many teachers, in order to avoid embarrassment and to maintain the appearance of power, restrict the computer's use to that of a mere drill machine for simple mechanical and memory skills. The computer thus becomes the world's most expensive flash card.

- Some teachers resist the use of computer games because the children seem to be having too much fun. Obviously, they cannot be learning. Some instructors only let the good students play the games.

- School administrators continue to believe that computers are too expensive. They have huge budgets and spend millions of dollars on school buildings and payrolls. One very small line item on the budget is called "course materials." If administrators view computers like books, there will never be enough money in the course material budget for computers.

- Computers are viewed by many teachers in the same light as movie projectors. Both are nice to have to supplement the activities of the school day, but neither is thought to be essential to the teaching process.

Only a few schools use computers as a primary method of teaching or maybe we should say as a primary method of tutoring. These situations will be discussed in Chapter 11. Unfortunately, the computer does not now represent a breakthrough in education in most schools, but it will in future years if the lessons outlined in this book are implemented. A few educators believe that we cannot truly have a breakthrough in education until we learn how to use technology as a personal tutoring system.

ARE WE SPENDING TOO MUCH ON EDUCATION?

This question was asked on the cover of *Forbes* magazine in December, 1986. The vast majority of educators say we are not spending enough on education. The *Forbes* story was a bold and creative article that dared to raise the opposite view. The facts that *Forbes* used were alarming because they clearly demonstrated that the cost of education was going up while the quality of education was going down. Here are a few statements drawn from the article:

- The Congressionally mandated National Assessment of Education Progress published its *Writing Report Card.* It stated that American school kids cannot write very well. The head of a large educational organization responded in the press by saying smaller classes (which are very costly) would give teachers more time to teach writing. Now the plain fact is that pupil-teacher ratios have been falling throughout this century. There were about 18 pupils per teacher in public schools in 1986. There were 27 in 1955. Back in 1900 there were 37. The magazine claims that education researchers have been unable to produce any consistent evidence that low pupil-teacher ratios actually do improve student performance.
- The ratio of pupils to the number of administrators and other professionals employed in the school system has decreased from 25.3 to 1 in 1955/56 to 15.9 to 1 in 1985/86. This decrease helps drive up the cost of education.
- The cost of education per year for each pupil increased from $1,000 in 1952 to $3,800 in 1986. This rise is not due to inflation, because the study used constant 1986 dollars.
- The SAT combined scores decreased from over 950 to slightly over 900 during the same period of time.
- The Secretary of Education in the Reagan administration, William Bennett, suggested there should be a "college cost containment" to match "hospital cost containment." Public and private college tuition and fees are rising 14.5% and 29.3% above the inflation rate.
- Economist Eric A. Hanushek of the University of Rochester concluded

that the experience since 1960 is unmistakable: "Expenditures are un-
related to school performance as schools are currently operated."
- U.S. education is essentially a socialized business, the American equivalent of the Soviet Union's collectivized farms.

Now, to summarize all these negative facts and figures into some
conclusions that will allow readers to move into the balance of the
book, where they will find the solutions to many of these key issues.

First, the cost of education is undoubtedly one of the two great
problems facing the education industry. Declining enrollments in most
communities are masking the ever-increasing cost of education, but
all parents of college-age children know that the cost of education
is rising at a faster rate than inflation. Yet, almost all solutions that
have been offered to the current crisis regarding quality in education
have recommended spending more money.

The recent emphasis on education and the "reform movement"
in education has brought huge sums of additional funds into the
process. Business, in its partnership with school systems during the
past five years, deserves an A plus for helping to obtain more funds
for education. This movement toward additional funding will slow
down sometime in the 1990s because the school systems are not
(with rare exceptions) increasing the quality of their product, that is,
educated students. The taxpayers and parents of college students will
soon realize that schools are not getting better, just more expensive.
Albert Shanker, president of the American Federation of Teachers,
said, "If all the reform reports of the last three years were adopted,
schools would look like the schools of the 1950's. The recent reform
effort, which has been good, has merely been aimed at correcting the
abuses of the 1960's."

THE OTHER MAJOR PROBLEM—QUALITY

If the *cost* of education is one of the two great problems facing
education systems, the other great problem must certainly be the
quality of education.

As the president of the College Board, Donald Stewart, has noted,
there have been hundreds of task forces to develop reform proposals.
Forty-five states have strengthened requirements for a standard high
school diploma, and most states have reassessed their policies on the
teaching profession, including certification, recognition, promotion,
and compensation. Thirty-seven states have acted to create career

ladders. But, as he also pointed out, it is business as usual in the overwhelming majority of classrooms. He cited limited evidence of a turnaround based on the findings of the National Assessment of Education Progress, the best measurement of the achievements of U.S. students aged 9, 13, and 17 in reading, math, and writing as well as in science, social studies, literature, music, art, and career development. Too often, the education reform movement has tried to improve the system without making changes in the classroom. In the 1990s, if there is to be a breakthrough in education, the process of education—of what happens in the classroom—must be restructured.

Another area of education that is affected by two major problems of cost and quality is employee education. Most people have no idea that employee education is a $40-billion-plus industry in the United States. Millions of employees attend school for a few days or weeks each year during their 30-to-40 year careers. The cost of education has been rising and many executives are becoming concerned not only about the cost but about the quality of education. In the next chapter, you will learn that great changes are taking place in the world of employee education to address these two major issues:

- How to raise the quality of education
- How to contain or reduce the cost of education

The lessons learned within employee education could become the model for restructuring the process of education in the public school and other education systems.

2 ///

Where Education Is Being Restructured

At a time when we desperately need breakthroughs in every area of education, many education organizations see their mission, consciously or unconsciously, as that of defending the "basics of education," which is essentially another way of saying "business as usual." Among the powers bolstering the status quo are these:

- Accreditation agencies, which ensure that educational institutions meet standards based on business-as-usual measurements
- Professional education organizations and teachers' unions, which too often in the past appear to have defended the status quo as defined from their own points of view
- Parents' organizations, which usually insist on a "back to the basics" approach and which want schools to be exactly as they remember them
- Colleges of education, whose curricula are typically based on certification procedures that maintain business-as-usual methods of teaching
- Boards of education, which are tremendously influenced by teachers' organizations, parents' groups, and accreditation agencies, and which are often so focused on day-to-day tactical issues that they do not spend time thinking about strategic change in the process of learning

In the meantime, government agencies, not-for-profit organizations, and profit-making companies are spending in excess of $40 billion a year on employee education. They are not inhibited by accreditation agencies, professional education organizations, school boards, or colleges of education. In fact, most of these professional education organizations have taken little interest in the employee-education departments of major businesses because employee education has been viewed as job training rather than as education.

EXAMPLES OF BREAKTHROUGHS IN RESTRUCTURING EDUCATION

Major educational breakthroughs are taking place in not-for-profit organizations, government agencies, and profit-making companies. Here are some examples:

- A systematic approach to designing courses, commonly referred to as *instructional design*, has evolved over the last 20 years. This approach has been demonstrated to be successful in producing courses that ensure more learning, more retention, and more application than courses left to be developed by individual instructors in their hours away from the classroom. Instructional design methods have a direct impact on reducing the cost of education while simultaneously raising its quality.
- Measurement of student performance is key to effective instructional design and is used to ensure more learning and retention. This is a significant reason why instructional design can impact the quality of education.
- Job aids that transfer the lessons learned in the classroom to the workplace for greater on-the-job productivity are being widely used.
- In some organizations, thousands of student days have been transferred from the traditional classroom to individual learning through self-study and computer-based training. One computer company is saving more than $200 million a year with this breakthrough while simultaneously increasing the quality of education.
- One new approach to interactive learning using computers in the classroom has increased learning by 40 percent.
- The skills of master teachers are being transmitted to remote classrooms through satellite communication systems, thus reducing the cost of education and increasing the quality.

- New videodisc systems tied to personal computers are bringing a new level of quality to education.

All these improvements in education will be discussed in more detail in the next nine chapters.

WHY IS RESTRUCTURING IMPORTANT?

When organizations are spending millions of dollars on education, they want to be sure that employees learn, retain, and apply the lessons taught. The following ten reasons for the growth of education within business and government organizations provide great motivation for improving the quality of education while containing its cost.

1. More sophisticated business processes

The simple typewriter and other basic tools of business have been replaced by computer terminals. If airline reservation agents are not thoroughly trained on a reservation system, they cannot sell a single ticket. More and more jobs require intensive training because of their expanded responsibilities.

2. Multiple jobs for each employee

More and more organizations are recognizing the need to cross-train employees for several jobs, thus permitting greater utilization of expensive workers during workload peaks and valleys. This is especially true for production workers in manufacturing plants.

3. Rewards for employee productivity

As computer systems are more widely used, a greater number of employees are measured on their performance in the way that manufacturing and sales personnel have been measured in the past. Outstanding workers welcome the recognition and the merit increases that such measurement can bring. They also want to be trained to a level that permits above-average performance.

4. Constant change

In the "good old days," a company would make and/or sell a line of products and services that would be basically the same for years. Now, companies are constantly announcing new goods and services, the production and provision of which require new training. For example, banks and insurance companies have doubled and even tripled the number of financial services they offer. Advancing technology in office and manufacturing equipment also adds to training requirements.

5. Customer education

The computer industry provides a good example of how to sell products through educating customers to make the right buying decisions. Customer personnel are also trained to install complex information systems. Every product announcement, therefore, increases the education requirements.

6. Employee mobility

People used to graduate from high school or college and then take a lifetime position with an organization. Today, most people will work for several companies during their 30 to 40 years of employment, and many will hold 10 to 15 jobs during that time. Being trained for new positions is now a way of life for most people throughout their working careers.

7. Full employment

Fewer companies today practice full employment, that is, a policy forbidding layoffs unless an employee cannot do a job or is unethical. Within companies that do practice full employment, there is a constant need to retrain employees for new jobs.

8. Promotion from within

Some companies have an extra workload of training because they do not hire managers and executives from outside the organization. Controllers, plant managers, sales managers, personnel managers, and so on must all be advanced from entry level positions and trained, over the years, for new responsibilities.

9. Desire to be a competitive candidate

Many employees want to influence their careers by becoming more competitive candidates for various jobs. Satisfying this desire requires additional education and training. Some organizations encourage their workers to grow through employee development courses during the day and tuition-refund programs that cover the cost of courses taken in the evenings or on weekends.

10. Remedial training

As job requirements expand, many employees do not have the basic reading, writing, and mathematical skills to take on the new responsibilities. This situation means that many organizations must now offer remedial courses.

EMPLOYEES AS A STRATEGIC RESOURCE

In their book *Reinventing the Corporation,* John Naisbitt and Patricia Aburdene write that, in the new information society, human capital has replaced dollar capital as the strategic resource. People and profits are inexorably linked. Dramatic changes are taking place in the education departments of major organizations, many of which employ thousands of staff, including instructors, course developers, computer support personnel, administrative people, and education technology experts. More education departments are being headed by executives with the title of vice president. The education department is integrally involved with the strategic planning of the organization. Education is now viewed as an essential part of the business, not as a sideshow that can be cut back or eliminated when profits decrease.

The American Society for Training and Development (ASTD) has published a report on education within government agencies and profit-making companies that helps us to understand why these dramatic changes are occurring. The 1986 report makes the following points:

- Employee training by employers is the largest delivery system for adult education.
- It is training and not formal education that provides most job skills.
- Formal education accounts for only a 15 percent variation in lifetime earnings, compared to 85 percent generated by workplace learning.
- Of the 40 million new jobs created in the past 15 years, only five to six million were in high-technology areas. The real challenge to training is the need to reskill America's workers for an information age and a service economy. By the year 2000, 75 percent of all workers currently employed will need retraining.
- Several million American workers are covered by union bargaining agreements that contain components for education and training.
- In the past five years, employee participation in training programs has increased and the number of training professionals has increased as well. These programs, now quite enormous in size and scope, have

been building since the 1940's. But because they were delivered by no single institution, were not the subject of a specific law or policy, and went on quietly and efficiently, they grew invisibly.

The ASTD report also showed how corporations are not only providing more education and training but also redesigning the nature of the courses they provide. Numerous companies, including exemplars such as General Electric and Xerox, report a major reorientation toward "needs-driven" education and training. Instead of providing a patchwork of unconnected training courses covering topics deemed "nice to know," companies are developing training programs tied to their strategic goals. Courses are more practical, building skills rather than just providing information. GE, for example, is "getting tough on the soft issues of culture, motivation and leadership in order to win in a global marketplace." Developmental programs for managers at GE's Crotonville, New York, facility reflect that goal. Managers receive training in global competition and in GE's entrepreneurial culture, in addition to training in management, marketing, finance and other functional courses.

THE ROLE OF MEASUREMENTS

Measurements are the essential element in achieving an increase in the quality of education while containing its costs. A situation I was personally involved in may help illustrate this point.

While my son was attending college at a major university, he one day asked me if I wanted to attend a class with him. Needless to say, I was thrilled that he had asked me to see what his class on international issues was like. He assured me that it was taught by an experienced teacher with the rank of full professor and that this would be a good class to sit in on.

When the professor walked into the classroom, he carried a manila folder full of lecture notes and newspaper clippings. He opened the folder and said, "Our lesson today is on disarmament. Who would like to start the discussion on arms control?" As usual, most students hesitated to ask questions or initiate discussion. Finally, the professor was able to get a little discussion going. Halfway through the class, I realized that the professor had no lesson plan and that he had made only the most minimal effort to prepare for the class. His answers to basic questions were weak. I was shocked when one of the students asked, "Where are the American missiles?" and the professor replied,

"I believe most are in the West somewhere. In fact, I think there are some in Wyoming."

Frankly, the students would have learned more by reading a good article in a newsmagazine or a leading newspaper. When I reflected on this incident, I couldn't help but think that a lack of measurement played a role in the performance of this full professor. Consider the following:

- He never took attendance, so the message to the students was clear. Being in class is not necessary or important.
- The students are not skilled in how to evaluate the professor's performance, and, even if they were, his tenured position would mean that their opinions would have little impact.
- No measurement will be taken on whether the students ever use the lessons. A few tests will be administered to see if the students have memorized some facts and figures.
- The dean of the school will never attend the class to review the professor's performance.
- The parents, who are paying the tuition, will probably never know anything about his performance.
- His pay, which I estimate at $50,000, is most likely not significantly influenced by his teaching performance.
- The only measurement to which the professor is subject is that he must be in class for three hours each week over a 15-week period and must give a final grade to each student. That really isn't much job pressure.

Across the campus was another teacher with the rank of full professor who earned $250,000. Yes, you guessed it, the football coach. Before anyone starts the usual argument about how terrible it is that a football coach makes five times what an academic professor makes, it's reasonable to look at some of the measurements to which the coach is subject.

- He will be measured on how well he teaches the knowledge and skills of football to his students, who are the players.
- Not only will he be measured on how well the players learn the plays, he will also be measured on how well they apply that learning to the job—the game held each Saturday afternoon. There is a defined, validated need to learn the lessons. The students must perform.

- He is measured on the number of seats sold, the revenue of the football season, the expense control of his program, and the overall performance of the team during the season.
- He must manage a staff of assistant coaches, and he probably faces every type of personnel problem that could possibly happen in any organization.
- Finally, he is measured on how well the alumni and fans like him personally, because he can have a great impact on the overall reputation of the school.

If other college professors expect to narrow the gap between their incomes and the income of a football coach, they must develop a measurement system that clearly demonstrates that their students learn and retain lessons and can apply them to the job better and that they can successfully compete in these abilities with students at other schools.

Measurement is what drives up the quality and reduces the cost of education in many organizations. Let me describe two "worlds" of education that I have seen in corporations to illustrate how important measurements are.

First, there is the *unstructured* world of education, where the measurements are these:

1. Do the students like the course? (Normally the students fill out a questionnaire at the end of the course.)
2. Are the classes full?
3. Can the education department charge out the expenses to line management?
4. How many students completed the course? (Sometimes referred to as *student days.*)

In this situation, no measurement is made of whether the students learn the lessons, retain them, or apply the lessons to the job. Thus, there is no measurement of the quality of education. The measurements all concern the quantity of education. The typical education manager soon realizes that having a large lecture hall full of students with an inexpensive instructor or videotape conducting the lessons is the way to raise the apparent productivity of the education department. In the world of unstructured education the real focus is on how much information can be communicated to how many people. In the long run, this type of education has very little value for any organization or employee.

Most organizations are now beginning to realize that their large budgets for education employees pay for too many unstructured courses. Therefore, many are evolving away from unstructured toward *structured* education. The key elements of structured education are these:

- Key jobs are identified within the organization.
- A curriculum of courses exists for each major job.
- Courses are developed to meet specific business needs.
- Managers and workers are provided with easy-to-understand guidelines for employee training rather than with a thick catalog containing descriptions of several hundred courses, which neither the manager nor the employee can readily comprehend.
- Courses are developed by instructional designers to reduce course-length, increase the amount of learning, provide job aids for applying the lessons, and increase the quality of education.
- Cost-effective delivery systems are implemented.
- Measurements of how well students learn, retain, and apply the lessons are incorporated into the courses.

The overall objective in the corporate classroom is to provide structured education throughout the organization, resulting in the right employee attending the right class at the right time. This movement from unstructured to structured education may sound simple and straightforward, but it actually represents a great revolution, a massive shift away from the traditional education system. The "how to" lessons that allow an organization to move away from unstructured toward structured education will be discussed in great detail during the next several chapters of the book.

SOME EXAMPLES OF OUTSTANDING EDUCATION

People sometimes ask the question, "Where are the organizations that have outstanding education programs?" The simple answer to this question is to look at the leading organizations within each industry. There you will usually find the most outstanding education programs. The reason is clear: To be successful an organization must have a defined mission, the right strategies for achieving its goals, and a solid education organization that gives employees effective training. Here are a few examples.

Ford Motor Company has an outstanding education program. On the first page of its course catalog, Ford tells its employees the mission of the company. Then the catalog discusses the values that Ford's education program promotes: *people* (who must be trained), *products,* and *profits.* The second page contains a letter from Ford's chief executive officer, with this message for the employees:

> At Ford, we recognize that the professional development of our employees is a key factor in the success of the company. We face new challenges every day to keep pace with changing technologies, markets, and competitors. Meeting these challenges will require highly skilled and trained employees who will provide fresh ideas and innovative approaches which contribute to Ford's growth. Ford education and training opportunities are designed for the mutual benefit of employees and the company.

The *Ford Education and Training Catalog* lists more than 200 company-sponsored courses, workshops, seminars, and programs. Courses are offered in such areas as

- Employee relations
- General engineering
- Computer/information systems
- Manufacturing engineering
- Product engineering
- Manufacturing
- Management and supervisory training
- Sales/marketing
- Secretarial/clerical
- Supply/purchasing
- Vehicle service
- Business/personal skills
- Facilitation skills
- Robotics
- Statistical methods

Xerox Corporation has 960 rooms at its large central education center in Leesburg, Virginia. Xerox's rise to leadership in the copier business required an outstanding education organization.

Up until the time of its divestiture AT&T spent more money on employee education than any other company. AT&T continues to have one of the most professional education departments of any corporation.

GTE, based in Norwalk, Connecticut, has an outstanding management development center. GTE is an organization that consists of what had originally been many different companies. The new center was built to bring an overall corporate culture to this diverse group of companies.

The Walt Disney organization has for years been a leader in the entertainment industry. Disney gives 340 orientation classes a year, and each new employee receives 12 hours of training before beginning work in one of Disney's theme parks. Disney employees are not called employees, but "cast members," and they are trained to help the visitors, who are called "guests." For example, when a "cast member" sees a father taking a photo of his family, he or she is trained to walk up to him and say, "Wouldn't you like to be in the picture, too?" Then the employee proceeds to take a photo of the entire family. The training pays off: 49 percent of all Disney guests come back every two years. Disney also has an outstanding management development program.

The FBI Academy is one of the reasons the FBI is so highly regarded as a leading law enforcement agency. This education center uses the latest in video techniques to train thousands of law enforcement officers.

Military education organizations have been leaders in the development of instructional design techniques as well as cost-effective delivery systems. Of course, they are faced by the challenge of having to train millions of people. U.S. military training programs have a great impact on other countries because they train thousands of foreign military personnel as well.

The United Way of America has an outstanding education organization called The Institute of Volunteerism, housed in Alexandria, Virginia, which provides training for thousands of executives and employees who work in not-for-profit organizations.

The leading insurance companies have outstanding marketing and management programs. Insurance is a people-oriented business, and well-trained personnel are what distinguish one insurance company from another. Banks, too, have had to implement large and extensive training programs because of automation and the expansion of the banking business into many new financial services.

The Marriott Corporation has grown to be the leading hotel and catering organization in the United States. Marriot accomplished this through an above-average investment in training for its employees. Holiday Inns has a large education center to train its innkeepers. The founder of Holiday Inns tells people that the rapid expansion and success of his chain was only possible because of the school that he created near Memphis, Tennessee.

Leading airlines like American, United, and Delta have built the industry through employee training. Pilot training is probably the most comprehensive and intensive training of all. Who would argue with the need for pilots to be 100-percent trained? A few organizations are beginning to apply concepts drawn from pilot training to other jobs. Executives are beginning to say, "We want all employees to do the job right 100 percent of the time."

IBM stands as an outstanding example of an organization that invests hundreds of millions of dollars each year on the education of its employees. In fact, taken together, IBM's education programs are almost as large as a state university program. IBM education executives provide direction to 7,000 instructors, course developers, and administrators who provide education to 390,000 employees in 130 countries. Raising the quality of education and delivering education in a cost-effective manner is a full-time effort at IBM.

EMERGENCE OF A NEW INDUSTRY

As large corporations, government agencies, and other organizations have expanded their education programs, another significant group of companies has formed to support them. A few hundred companies now exist whose business is to develop courses for corporate class-rooms. About a hundred of these companies belong to an organization called the Instructional Systems Association (ISA). Founded in 1978 by the chief executive officers of several training firms, ISA seeks to advance the common good of the training industry by promoting research, development, and scholarship in instructional systems. Several thousand outstanding educators now work for these companies. These educators are on the leading edge of instructional design, offering new methods of teaching, new delivery systems, and new systems for developing courses. Why are they on the leading edge?

Their courses must sell in the marketplace. Their courses are constantly being measured and evaluated, and new methods of learning must be successful or the courses will not sell. If you want to see the results of competition within education, look at this new industry, which today has many of the attributes of a cottage industry. Some of the most creative and dedicated education professionals work for these companies. Their salaries are often twice as high as those earned by schoolteachers or college instructors, because their performance is being measured. Some of the owners and executives of the larger companies are earning as much money as the football coach described earlier. Competition does wonderful things for the field of education.

SUMMARY

This chapter has discussed the outstanding education programs developed by leading organizations. What about the organizations and industries that have never invested a sufficient amount of resources for employee training? The railroad and steel industries, among many other basic manufacturing enterprises, are prime examples. International competition has provided the final blow to some of these companies, which short-changed themselves by refusing to invest in training for their employees.

Some traditional educators, after having quickly surveyed employee education, have immediately come to the conclusion that corporations are only providing basic job-training. What these educators have overlooked is that basic job-training in most companies today must address the challenges raised by sophisticated tasks—and that these challenges call for complex educational processes whose success can be accurately measured. These traditional educators should take time to perform an in-depth study of the education organizations described in this chapter. They would find the following:

- Millions of dollars are being spent on education research to determine how lessons will be learned, retained, and applied to the job.
- Millions are being spent on developing interactive methods of learning that are far superior to the traditional lecture-based methods of teaching.
- Thousands of instructional designers are practicing their new knowledge and skills in developing courses that are far superior to the traditional courses that exist in public schools and universities.
- Major efforts are being implemented to improve the measurement of education so that the millions of dollars spent in corporate classrooms can be justified.
- Millions of dollars are being spent on cost-effective delivery

systems, such as computer-based training (CBT) and CBT with videodisc simulations.

- A number of organizations are investing in new methods of instructor training and development. Some of these organizations are building a curriculum of courses to train more instructional designers. A few companies even have customized courses for developing managers of education, who go on to direct multimillion-dollar education centers.
- Millions of dollars are being invested in new education centers that use the leading edge of technology to provide motivational courses for their employees.
- Thousands of instructors are earning $35,000 to $75,000 a year, with a high degree of job satisfaction.
- Course developers and instructional designers are earning up to $85,000 as they demonstrate that their new courses cost less to administer while ensuring that students learn the lessons.

This is the revolution that is taking place within employee education today. It will result in organizations being able to determine precisely what students need to know to be able to perform their jobs. Course content will be of the highest quality. Students will enjoy learning, and will understand the need to acquire new knowledge and skills. Instruction will be delivered through different methods, such as self-study, personal tutoring, and in classrooms with highly-qualified teachers. Series of exercises along the road to learning will ensure that students master the lessons. Almost every student *will* master them. Encouragement and praise will replace humiliation from impatient teachers. This is the world of education that students, teachers, and administrators want to work in. All this is feasible today and is currently being practiced in some education departments.

The restructuring of education started in the 1970s and is moving at an accelerated pace in the 1980s. Explosive growth will occur for employee education in the 1990s as more and more organizations realize the value of trained employees. After all, the cost of an untrained employee is enormous:

- If an employee cannot do a job, the simple answer is to hire more employees, which raises the cost of labor.
- Untrained employees make many costly errors.
- Untrained employees are the cause of sloppy or incomplete work. Recent emphasis on quality within the United States has made

clear the high cost of testing, re-work, and quality control departments.

- Untrained employees are unhappy and usually unmotivated, so they set the terrible tone of doing as little as possible to get by.

SRI International, a leading consulting firm, performed a study of corporate education and training. The opening paragraph of its executive summary reports:

> The role and strategic importance of corporate-sponsored education and training has undergone a fundamental shift in the past few years as corporations have sought new means to deal with new business challenges. Corporate education and training has evolved from a fairly routine, technically necessary but strategically insignificant activity to a potentially important source of competitive advantage. It is increasingly being used as a strategic tool for firms to use in dealing with critical issues of competitiveness and significant changes in business environment. Today, corporate education and training is becoming an important tool for top management, a new lever to help manage the corporation in a time of rapid change, and a new means of competing more effectively in today's technologically sophisticated and globally oriented economy.

An entire book could be written on the success stories of education within government agencies, not-for-profit organizations, and profit-making companies, but that is not the intent of this book. The purpose of this book is to tell *how* these organizations are restructuring their education systems. The next nine chapters will outline what it takes to build a successful education program.

The book's final five chapters will take the lessons learned in the corporate classrooms and apply those lessons to public schools, colleges and universities, and continuing adult education programs. One of the key elements of a successful education program is the active participation and support of the executive management that leads the organization. How do you obtain this leadership and participation? The answers are in the next chapter.

PART 2 ///

RESTRUCTURING EMPLOYEE EDUCATION: A SUCCESS STORY

3 ///

How to Obtain Executive Interest in Education

Executives *are* interested in education. They themselves have attended grammar school, high school, universities, employee training programs, and executive development courses. They often serve on school boards, and they frequently have an opportunity to be education task-force members. They, like all of us, are frustrated by the ever-increasing cost of education and the lack of tangible results from existing education programs.

But despite their interest and frequent involvement in education, too many executives today assume that the employees who work for them have been trained to do their jobs. Executives must ask three key questions if they are even to begin to understand the health of the education function in their organizations.

1. Have jobs been clearly defined?
2. Are employees trained to do their jobs?
3. Are there measurements for job performance?

Too often a job description system that uses vague generalities and a performance management system that also uses broad general statements are considered answers to these three important questions. Many executives admit that they don't spend more than ten minutes a year reviewing their companies' training programs. The management attention they give to educating and training their employees is often limited to reducing the firm's training budget if it appears to be growing too rapidly. They manage education in this offhand way despite their awareness that engineers become obsolete every few years, their own frequent decisions to change products and strategies, and the many other factors that require employees to be constantly retrained to meet new job performance requirements.

A few executives do give careful consideration to the three questions listed above and carefully inspect the answers they receive. They fully understand that if jobs are not defined down to the level of task analysis, their workers are probably doing less than the total that a job requires. These executives refuse to accept general courses on time management, stress management, and effective communication as comprising a complete employee-training program. They insist, instead, on courses being directed to the specific job requirements.

TRAINING AS AN INVESTMENT

Most executives view education and training programs primarily as an expense. This view allows increases in education budgets only during years of revenue and profit growth and demands drastic cuts during business downturns. Until recently, only a few companies treated education as an investment. One of these is Arthur Andersen & Co., a leading public accounting and consulting firm. Years ago, Andersen's managing partners decided to invest in an education program that today includes the world's largest employee-education center, located in St. Charles, Illinois, outside of Chicago. The center provides training for about 1,600 auditors, tax specialists, and consultants each week. In addition, thousands of student days, in which employees take self-study or computer-based training courses, are offered at Andersen's local offices around the world.

The partners of Arthur Andersen are convinced that hiring outstanding college graduates and then providing them with the firm's own in-depth training results in a professional staff that works more rapidly, at a lower price, and at a higher level of quality than would otherwise be possible. Andersen's growth over the past 20 years supports its management's conviction that investment in training and developing the firm's professional staff pays off.

IBM, Digital Equipment Corporation (DEC), Xerox, AT&T, and other members of the information and communications industries have also treated education as an investment rather than an expense. This view has been a major factor in the explosive growth enjoyed by these companies during the past several decades. In companies that continue to view education as an expense, the executive team needs to be briefed on the difference between unstructured education, which *is* often just an expense, and structured education, which is an investment.

STRUCTURED EDUCATION AS AN INVESTMENT

A review of the definition of unstructured education will allow us to see why it is almost always an expense and very rarely an investment. First, in almost every organization that uses an unstructured approach, hundreds of courses have accumulated over the years for various reasons. The quality of the course content and the instruction varies widely. Second, although there are usually large catalogs to explain the courses, line management is not generally integrally involved in course selection. The employee decides which course to take, and may do so for a variety of reasons, ranging from "I need it for my job" to "I am bored with my job and a few days at the company education center will be a real break." Finally, an unstructured education system encourages the use of classes as a form of reward. Line management tells a worker, "Take a few days off and attend a course because you have been working hard." Unfortunately, managers also often use courses as a way of dealing with problem employees, who are always in school because managers would rather not have them back on the job. Clearly, programs as poorly managed as this are a waste of money and nothing but an expense.

These undesirable aspects of weak education programs can be eliminated by evolving to a structured education system, which demands answers to new questions:

1. Are the courses related to a true business requirement?
2. Have the courses been developed to minimize the time away from the job?
3. Do the courses include exercises that ensure that students learn and retain the lessons?
4. Are the students provided with job aids to transfer the learning to the job?

Managers and supervisors should receive guidelines on the curriculum of courses for each job. These permit line management to design an annual development and training program for each employee. The goal is to make each employee more productive as well as to develop some employees for jobs of greater responsibility.

COST AS A WAY TO CAPTURE EXECUTIVE ATTENTION

Training directors often complain that their programs are little more than a side show within their organizations. Like the comedian Rodney Dangerfield, they "never get any respect." They cannot convince executive management to focus on education. Their big question is, "How do we get the executives involved with education?" Many directors of education will say, "Tell the executives about all the good courses, but never divulge the overall cost of education." But frankly, if you really want to bring executive focus to education, the cost figures will make it happen faster than anything else you can tell them.

The IBM management team, for example, realized it was spending large sums on various education programs. When they were shown that worldwide education programs within IBM were costing $900 million per year they really wanted to sharpen their focus on education. Everyone sits up straight in the boardroom chairs when you show the true cost of education. But determining the actual costs of education is a big challenge. The expenses are spread throughout the organization. You must gather and add up small numbers from hundreds or thousands of department budgets. Some people claim it's as complicated as adding fractions. Most cost studies start by looking for the numbers in the accounting system, but this approach only represents a start and will rarely be successful by itself.

Within IBM, we first had to identify all the major areas of education in the company. Then we asked the plans and controls managers of each education department to write a report that included

1. How many people are there in education?

   – Managers (includes executives and supervisors)
   – Instructors
   – Course developers
   – Education specialists
   – Computer support personnel
   – General administrative personnel
   – Class administrative personnel

2. What are the costs in the major areas of expense?

   - Salaries of full-time education personnel
   - Salaries of part-time instructors
   - Fees paid to outside instructors
   - Course development expenses
   - Staff travel and living expenses
   - Student travel and living expenses
   - Course materials (books, papers, etc.)
   - Administrative support
   - Computer support
   - Rent or depreciation of facilities
   - Utilities
   - General overhead

3. What courses are being taught (broken down by major delivery systems, such as classroom or self-study)?

   - Number of student completions
   - Number of student days

The plans and controls managers were asked to remove any expenses that were not directly related to education. For example, if computer-room expense was included in their statements but only 50 percent of computer-time was devoted to education, they were instructed to include only 50 percent of the computer room charges. On the other hand, if, for example, the education-center administrative staff was paid for out of the headquarters' budget, the money spent on those administrative personnel was to be included in the cost study.

The cost study—for a company with almost 400,000 employees spread over 130 countries—was completed within 60 days. It showed that the cost of employee education was 50 percent higher than a study conducted a few years earlier had estimated.

EFFECTIVELY POSITIONING THE COST OF EDUCATION

Most organizations underestimate employee education costs and training by a wide margin. By keeping the costs hidden, many directors of education feel they are protecting their instructors and education centers. The opposite is usually the case. The organizations that have the most complete and professional education programs know exactly what their costs are. Outstanding education executives also use the cost of education to raise the quality of education.

Once you know the cost of education, the presentation to executive management must be carefully developed to avoid the normal reactions:

- Do we need all that education?
- How good are those courses?
- Couldn't we reduce the expenses by 25 percent?
- What would the impact be if we stopped most of those courses for a year?

Directors of education have a difficult time answering these questions because they are not easy to answer. Therefore, in order to deal with these penetrating questions before they are asked, a plan of action must be presented with the cost-study figures so that the executives can see how resources will be managed.

Here is an outline of how a successful presentation to executive management might work:

1. Show the business need for education and training programs within the organization.
2. Present a plan to evolve from an unstructured to a structured education system, with new measurement requirements.
3. Present a plan to raise the quality of education.
4. Show how cost-containment programs for education can be implemented.
5. Lay out a plan for a new management system.
6. Show the need to perform an organization study.
7. Detail the size and scope of education today (cost study).
8. Recommend that an executive advisory board be set up.

THE EXECUTIVE ADVISORY BOARD

The last point in the list above—the recommendation for the advisory board—is extremely important. Motorola, which has approximately 100,000 employees, provides a good example of how such a board functions. In the 1980s the company established a new focus on education by building the Motorola Training and Education Center on the site of its corporate headquarters at a suburban location outside

Chicago. Motorola also hired a new vice president of training and education, who is one of the leaders within industrial education. The chief executive officer of Motorola, Robert Galvin, served as the chairman of a ten-person executive advisory board until he retired. The board continues to meet twice a year in the corporate boardroom. The board includes the senior executives in charge of major line organizations. One objective of the board is to be sure that the education programs support the strategic plans of the company. The board also reviews major new education programs as well as new delivery systems such as computer-based training.

The cost study gains attention and creates executive interest in education. The executive advisory board is the vehicle for establishing a long-term partnership between executive management and the education organization.

ENHANCING PARTNERSHIP WITH EXECUTIVE MANAGEMENT

After the cost study has been presented, the next meeting with executive management will usually occur from six to twelve months later. This meeting should present and sell the strategic directions of the education organization. Here is a sample agenda for such a meeting:

- Case study (10 minutes) of how one area of the business has evolved from an unstructured education system to a structured one.
- Case study (20 minutes) of how courses are professionally developed, focusing on the reduction of time away from the job as well on as how the course includes exercises to ensure that the student learns and retains the lessons and applies them to the job.
- Demonstration (20 minutes) of how courses are delivered in decentralized learning centers, reducing or eliminating the costs of education centers, instructor staffs, and student travel and living expenses.
- Summary (10 minutes) of how education can be managed this way throughout the organization if a central focus is established for education.

If this presentation is successful it will usually result in the creation of a study of how to organize education within the company. After a central focus has been established for education, the director or vice president of education should prepare a policy letter on education for the chief executive officer to sign. The letter signed by the CEO of IBM explained the responsibilities of the corporate education department, the corporate function staffs, and line management, and it included the following points:

- IBM's commitment to education for both customers and employees is essential to our long-term success.
- A new corporate education function has been formed to ensure focus on this important activity.
- Employees are responsible for seeking training and development.
- IBM managers are responsible for employee education planning to enhance employee performance and career growth.

Several years ago, I met with the senior vice presidents and other executives of the General Motors Corporation, who were developing a new strategic direction for employee training within their company. Their effort resulted in the publication of the *GM Philosophy of Training,* an outstanding document that clearly explains the importance of employee training to management and employees. Among the points emphasized in this document are the following:

The worldwide performance of General Motors is the result of the performance of each person in the Corporation. The purpose of training is to increase the effectiveness of individuals to enable them to contribute to the Corporation's mission and implement its guiding principles. Thus, the goal of training is of mutual benefit—for the individual and the Corporation. This is accomplished by enhancing employees' knowledge, skills and attitudes that have a positive impact upon job performance and to help them reach their fullest potential as members of the General Motors team.

Opportunities for improved performance exist at all levels of the organization. Managers in each unit are responsible for providing training based upon an assessment of the needs of individuals and the organization. The establishment of training priorities, in the exercise of sound managerial discretion, must be integrated with business planning. The Corporation has the responsibility for allocating financial and human resources for training. The employee shares the responsibility for individual career development with the Corporation.

Training is a continuing process and is an essential element of human resources development. Among those instances when it is important that training should be provided are

- When a person enters the organization.
- When a person is about to assume new job responsibilities.

- When a person's job performance requires improvement.
- When new conditions require changes in technology, products, policies, practices, and procedures.
- When a person leaves the organization due to the closing or indefinite suspension of an operation, to help secure other employment more readily.

The effectiveness of training will be measured by its contribution to the improvement of individual and organizational performance.

EDUCATION AS PART OF A PLANNING SYSTEM

Companies of all sizes have goals and strategies. Goals define where an organization wants to be at the end of a strategic period. The length of a strategic period may vary from three to ten years, but the average is probably five years. Strategies are the broad plans, or road maps, that describe how the organization will reach its goals over the strategic period.

Too often, an organization will put its book of goals and strategies on a shelf with the idea it should be reviewed once a year. This makes the development of goals and strategies a meaningless exercise, because they are not used for guiding the day-to-day decisions of the organization. If you want goals and strategies to have meaning, you must have annual action programs to support them. Once or twice a year, management should review the organization's major programs to see if they are moving along the appropriate roads (strategies) toward the defined goals.

Annual action programs, such as sales campaigns, usually have headcount and dollars associated with them, because such programs are typically a part of the annual budget process. In addition, there are capital dollars for building and equipment which are necessary to implement the action programs.

Very few companies take the critical next step, namely, to include education requirements as part of their management systems. You have to wonder how executives can think that action programs can be successfully implemented without their personnel being properly trained.

Once education requirements have been included in the management system, the final step should be to tie the performance management system into the overall management system. Individual performance is the basis for successful implementation of action programs and therefore personnel performance expectations are critical.

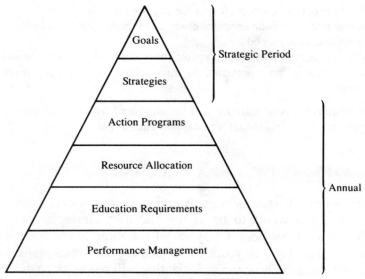

FIGURE 1. A management system.

Successful companies carefully define performance plans and make meaningful annual appraisals of their employees as a way of setting and meeting personnel performance expectations. Figure 1 depicts in a schematic way the management system of a successful organization, showing how educational requirements fit into the overall system.

EXAMPLES OF EDUCATION IN PLANNING SYSTEMS

A few case studies will help to illustrate how education can be successfully included in a management system as well as to show how costly mistakes can be made when education is not included.

A large computer company set a goal to lower the cost of marketing. One strategy for reaching that goal was to replace the company's three marketing divisions with two. Fortunately, the action programs that were set up to accomplish this included the millions of dollars needed to retrain marketing representatives and systems engineers on new products, applications, and customer responsibilities. If the training had not been provided, the reorganization would have been a disaster.

Everyone remembers the great success stories of personal-computer companies in the early 1980s. Several companies were enjoying explosive growth, and forecasters predicted that growth would continue for years to come. That the companies should continue to develop new hardware and software was seen as the only requirement for continued growth. To almost everyone's surprise, the personal-computer business hit a plateau in the mid-1980s. Too many personal computers had become dust collectors because of a lack of customer education on how to use this new technology.

Dozens of case studies could be drawn up to describe how organizations have failed to achieve growth plans or failed to make the major strategic changes that had been approved by executive management. Many excuses are offered. Most MBAs who write case studies never look at whether education requirements were included in action programs they analyze. Rarely do you write that a growth plan or strategic change failed because employees lacked adequate training to do the job. Yet all too often this is one of the major reasons for failure.

PERFORMANCE SYSTEMS: KEY TO THE FUTURE

Employee performance requirements will take on much greater meaning in the 1990s. Organizations will evolve from a generalized approach to performance management toward conducting detailed performance engineering studies for major jobs. The process will include three basic steps:

1. Establishing a model of the desired output
2. Establishing measurements for existing output
3. Developing strategies and action programs to bring each job's existing output up to the desired output

Measurements of output will become a major issue. The cost of labor and equipment is so high that new, accurate measurements will be needed to justify the huge investments required to support new growth and strategic plans.

Federal Express provides an interesting example of how a leading organization is acting to include education requirements in its overall management system. Fred Smith, the founder of Federal Express, has taken his quest for superior performance within his huge package-delivery company to a new level of investment. Reports indicate that Federal Express is spending over $20 million to build interactive video education programs to train a field organization of over 23,000 people to deliver a new level of customer service.

In the past, package delivery companies provided minimal training to those they hired. The usual training would consist of little more than showing new employees how to fill out forms and keep basic records. Then the trainee was given a route of customers and sent out with the comment, "Good luck in the new job." New employees ordinarily required several months of trial and error to fully learn their jobs. Customers would be unhappy with the errors, and the new employees would be unhappy with the unhappy customers. Many workers gave up after a few weeks of work.

In the meantime, Federal Express had invested millions of dollars in new airplanes, warehouses, automated distribution systems, and information systems to keep track of packages. Smith and his management team decided that the employees who picked up and delivered packages had to be as well trained as the pilots who flew Federal Express's planes. After all, the employees on pickup and delivery routes are the ones who encounter customers face-to-face. Their performance is a major factor in the value that customers place on the overall system.

Within two years, more than 6,000 customer-service agents and 17,000 couriers will be exposed to comprehensive education programs at their branch offices. These programs will include training that utilizes videodiscs running on personal computers.

A company will only make this type of investment in the training of its employees when executive management understands the value of employee training. In the 1950s and 1960s, consultants said that the future belonged to organizations in which executives understood the value of computers and installed comprehensive information systems. After spending billions of dollars on computers and new buildings, equipment, and processes, executive management should now be investing in employee training at the level that Federal Express is investing. Executive management must become as involved in employee training during the 1990s as it has been in computers and information systems during the past 30 years.

SUMMARY

A definite trend is developing in which senior executives of many organizations are taking leadership roles in education. The 1987 SRI report "Corporate Education and Training" states that, far more than before, chief executive officers and others in senior management are directly monitoring or participating in corporate education and training activities. GE officials estimate that the company's CEO,

Jack Welch, spends as many as 12 days a year on site at GE's corporate management development center in Crotonville, New York. Robert Galvin, head of Motorola, and John Filer, former CEO of Aetna, both helped establish new training institutes at their companies and hired the institute directors.

The amount of change that will occur within education organizations is greater than most people realize. Old, unstructured education systems will go the way of the one-room schoolhouse. New, structured education systems will require the central planning and leadership that will be described in the next several chapters of this book and that is an essential factor in the education revolution. This revolution requires the support of executive management. The lessons learned by organizations on the leading edge, lessons about how to create and implement partnerships with executive management, are essential to creating a new, structured education system in any organization.

4 ///

How to Contain the Cost of Education

Too often, when I speak on the management of employee education to audiences outside of IBM, I encounter the belief that IBM has unlimited resources to devote to any program, including education. Such people forget that a company does not become number one in profits by wasting money on "nice to do" projects. All the corporate functions within IBM, including education, contend for a limited amount of resources. If a new education center, costing $25 million, is constructed, that means some plant doesn't get built or that a new product development project is deferred. Executives are more interested in additional programmers, engineers, or marketing personnel than they are in funding more instructors. They are constantly asking if the resources for education can be reduced.

Once executives realize how much they are spending, their number one question is, "How do we contain the cost of education?" This is not an easy question to answer. Four elements of information are needed for a quick understanding of the size and expense of education within an organization:

1. Number of employees
2. Cost of labor and benefits
3. Average number of student days per employee
4. Delivery systems used within education

60

Table 1. Typical Labor Costs in Organizations of Various Size.

| | Labor Costs | |
Number of Employees in the Organization	Service Organization	High Technology Organization
100	$2,500,000	$4,000,000
1,000	$25,000,000	$40,000,000
5,000	$125,000,000	$200,000,000
10,000	$250,000,000	$400,000,000
50,000	$1,250,000,000	$2,000,000,000
100,000	$2,500,000,000	$4,000,000,000
200,000	$5,000,000,000	$8,000,000,000
400,000	$10,000,000,000	$16,000,000,000

QUICK ESTIMATE OF EDUCATION EXPENSE

The expense of education in any organization can be quickly estimated. Everyone knows that there is no such thing as an "inexpensive" employee. The average yearly cost of a full-time employee ranges from $25,000 to $40,000 (including salary and benefits) depending on the type of industry. Table 1 shows at a glance the typical cost of labor in companies of various size. The figures presented in Table 1 represent the fixed expense of having employees on board for one year. Once again, the question should be raised whether all these employees, who cost millions and billions of dollars, are fully trained to do their jobs. If they are, their company has a very large training and education budget. If they are not adequately trained, the company probably has more employees than necessary, which usually means its labor cost is much higher than that of a business that has an adequate training program.

Many companies average five days of training per year per employee while "high-tech" organizations often average ten days per employee. Table 2 gives the number of student days, or training volume, within organizations of various size. Now, how do student days translate into dollar costs? Suppose the class is offered at a local, onsite education center that requires no travel or living expenses. The typical cost is $150 per day per student, including rent or building

Table 2.   Number of Student Days in Organizations of Various Size.

	Number of Student Days	
Number of Employees in the Organization	5 Student Days per Employee	10 Student Days per Employee
100	500	1,000
1,000	5,000	10,000
5,000	25,000	50,000
10,000	50,000	100,000
50,000	250,000	500,000
100,000	500,000	1,000,000
200,000	1,000,000	2,000,000
400,000	2,000,000	4,000,000

depreciation, utilities, course materials, class administration, general administration, equipment, instructors, and management. A 20-person class will therefore cost $3,000 a day. If the course lasts five days, the cost will be $15,000. If the course is offered ten times a year, the cost will be $150,000. This simple exercise shows how fast an education budget can expand. Add to this the fact that courses offered by outside organizations often cost as much as $200 a day (with $50 being the marketing cost and the profit margin).

Of course, many organizations only count variable costs and not fixed costs such as the depreciation of an education center. For this reason many organizations underestimate their training costs and have little appreciation for the real expense involved.

Of course, many training programs are not provided at local education centers but are offered at central education centers, so that travel and living expenses must be figured into the costs of education. Depending on a center's location, travel and living costs will range from $100 to $200 per day per student. For a national organization, the typical cost is $350 per day for travel and living expenses and tuition ($150 tuition plus $200 travel and living). Now repeat the exercise above. If the course has twenty students and lasts for five days, its cost will be $35,000. If the course is offered 30 times a year, the budget for just one course will exceed a million dollars. Table 3 enables us to make a quick estimate of the cost of student days, based on varying percentages of local, onsite education and central education.

Table 3. Cost of Student Days

Number of Student Days	100% Local Student Days	50% Local, 50% Central Student Days	100% Central Student Days
5,000	$750,000	$1,250,000	$1,750,000
10,000	$1,500,000	$2,500,000	$3,500,000
50,000	$7,500,000	$12,500,000	$17,500,000
100,000	$15,000,000	$25,000,000	$35,000,000
500,000	$75,000,000	$125,000,000	$175,000,000
1,000,000	$150,000,000	$250,000,000	$350,000,000
2,000,000	$300,000,000	$500,000,000	$700,000,000
4,000,000	$600,000,000	$1,000,000,000	$1,400,000,000

Clearly, the costs of employee training are high. That is why I tell my course developers and instructors at IBM, "Every ten minutes must be outstanding." The key question is, "Are we getting the maximum return from our investments in employees and our investment in education?" Thus, I have devoted the entire next chapter to showing how the quality of education can be raised.

HOW EDUCATION COSTS GROW

The American Society For Training and Development, in a study performed several years ago, found the cost of formal employee training in the United States to be around $30 billion. Many people believe that that number will approach $50 billion as the 1980s come to an end. The cost of education is probably growing fastest in companies that still use an unstructured system. The following example shows how such growth can continue unchecked.

The director of education of a company sends out a survey each fall to all the first-line managers and supervisors, asking, "How much training do you need next year?" The survey reminds the managers that the tuition charge for each student is about $150 a day. The survey usually comes back with a request for 15 to 25 percent more training than had been requested the year before. Managers want their employees trained, and they insist they will somehow find the money. (Tuition charges do not appear to be much of a constraint on the growth of education.)

Next, the director informs the executives of the demand for the courses and uses the strong demand to prove that the education department is offering quality courses. The director claims that the line managers want education and that they are willing to pay for the increased courses and student volume. The director of education's argument is that, since all expenses will be charged back to line management, it is not he or she who is asking for an increased budget. Because the budgets of first-line managers almost never contain a line item for education, tuition will be charged to line items such as meetings, outside programs, employee development, and the ever-useful "miscellaneous." This traditional way of planning education eliminates any effective budget review by the executives. Fifteen percent is a representative average for the growth of education expenses when no central budget for education exists.

EIGHT STEPS TO COST CONTAINMENT

In the past few years, I have been able to identify eight steps for containing the cost of education.

The first step toward cost containment involves finding out how much is being spent on training and education within the organization. The previous section showed how to perform a cost study on education. Many companies will find they are spending millions—perhaps even hundreds of millions—of dollars on education. The pressure for additional education will always exist because of the increasing complexity of work and the burgeoning use of high technology in almost every kind of job. In addition, the massive pressures resulting from international competition, takeovers, and mergers increase the need for additional education programs.

The worst executive decision is to "take a meat ax" to the education budget through arbitrary reductions. A 25-percent across-the-board cut will usually damage both the education program and the company itself. Courses that are essential to running the organization will be cut. Too often, an executive decision to make a major cut in the education budget provides a very expensive lesson to the executives concerning how important trained employees are to the company's ability to meet the annual objectives.

The second step in cost containment is to determine how essential each course is to the overall education program and then to assign a code to it. Each organization must develop its own list of requirement codes, but here are the codes used at IBM:

Code   Description

1   Entry program for new hires or redeploys (start new employees)

2   Customer and systems engineer courses (protect the revenue)

3   New product or new service courses (protect the growth)

4   Essential job training (permit new assignments for employees)

5   Advanced development courses (protect promotion from within)

6   Discretionary courses (nice to do in good years)

Many companies will find that 20 to 30 percent of the courses they now offer belong in code 6; for some companies, this may be as high as 50 percent. The key to this step is to identify the essential courses for meeting revenue and profit goals and then to protect these courses from cutbacks.

The third step in cost containment is tradeoff planning, using the resources freed from code 6 courses to develop essential courses that are not presently being taught. Another element of tradeoff planning is to use newly available funds and resources in course development to increase individualized learning. Individualized learning, the big breakthrough in cost containment, will be described later in this chapter.

The fourth step in cost containment involves making sure that the right person takes the right class at the right time. This sounds simple, but the task is such a challenge that I have devoted Chapter 6 entirely to this subject. The point of this step is clear: Too many students are sitting in classes that do not offer the education they need.

The fifth step is to ensure that each course is developed only once. This is not necessarily a big problem for small and intermediate-size companies, but it is a major problem within large organizations. Computer literacy courses were developed independently 27 times in one large computer company! A basic electronics course was developed 14 times in another large manufacturing firm. Safety courses are usually developed at each plant site. Employee development courses, such as courses in time management and effective communications, are usually developed at least a dozen times.

The sixth step is to use instructional design techniques in developing courses. This subject is discussed in detail in the next chapter. A structured instructional design approach to course development will reduce course length. Consider the savings that can result: If one course-day is saved and there are 500 students in the class, the savings may reach $75,000. If 5,000 students are enrolled over the life of the course, the savings will be $750,000.

The seventh step is to emphasize the use of existing courses available from course-development companies or universities and junior colleges. While existing courses may not exactly match your needs, a 90-to-95 percent match can often be found. Do not waste money redeveloping existing courses merely to eliminate the 5 percent difference you think your organization requires.

The eighth and final step in cost containment is the use of cost-effective delivery systems. There are two basic delivery systems for education: classroom instruction and individualized learning. Although in many situations classroom instruction is the most appropriate choice, very often some form of individualized learning is clearly more cost-effective. In a large organization, identifying cost-effective delivery systems is the number one opportunity to achieve a breakthrough in the cost of education. Let's start by reviewing the least costly delivery system with individualized learning.

SELF-STUDY

Self-study courses originated in the 1950s, when the military developed a series of highly structured, programmed instruction manuals. The intent was to have soldiers and sailors learn basic tasks by reading these manuals. This approach offered several advantages over traditional, classroom-based approaches.

1. Education was available when a person needed the training.
2. No instructors were required, which saved money.
3. The costs of an education center and all the expensive support that such a center requires were eliminated.
4. Travel and living costs were eliminated.

Pilot tests of self-study showed that students could learn as much through this kind of individualized program as they would by listening to a teacher in a classroom if the information was of a fundamental and factual nature. A lecture-based course whose purpose was to convey basic information was the perfect kind of course to convert from classroom to self-study.

Businesses soon learned of this breakthrough in the cost of education. Companies tried self-study in the 1960s and 1970s, and some experienced real success using self-study techniques. In 1974, I was responsible for introducing self-study within the IBM sales training program. The first course took six months and cost $240,000 to design, used instructional design techniques, and integrated video and audio tapes with the print materials. Learning centered on the print materials, but the video and audio tapes supplemented the print curriculum by providing real-life examples and helped to keep the marketing representatives motivated. Before 1974 no one had ever spent as much as $240,000 to develop a course at IBM nor taken six months to do it. The course was much higher in quality than many previous efforts, however, and it was well received by the marketing force.

The money and time expended were easy to justify. The Data Processing Division of IBM employed approximately 4,000 marketing representatives in 1974. At 1974 prices, the cost for a typical classroom-based sales training program would have been $250 a day times 5 days times 4,000 students—or $5 million—because central education centers were required. Suddenly, $240,000 didn't seem like such a big figure. By comparison, a classroom course would have been developed by a task force in 30 days and would probably have included a lot of entertainment to keep up student morale, but it wouldn't have included as many lessons as the self-study course. The self-study course only took three days to administer, so some 8,000 days of selling effort were saved per year. All the statistics seemed positive. There was only one problem. The great limitations to self-study lie in the lack of predictable interaction between students and instruction materials and the difficulty of real-time measurements to gauge a self-study program's results. Some students will spend a couple of hours on a self-study course that is designed to take three days to complete and then say, "I know all that." The solution to this problem is a computer managed system that provides exercises and measures learning. This leads to the next step in individualized learning: computer-based training.

COMPUTER-BASED TRAINING

Computer-based training's big advantage is the potential for significant interaction between a personal computer and a student. Computer-based training programs can be designed so that a student must interact, *must do something.* Students cannot simply flip pages and announce they are finished.

Earlier, I said that I tell my instructors and course developers that every ten minutes must be outstanding. Computer-based training provides a great opportunity to assure that the training *is* outstanding. The course developer can examine every ten-minute instructional segment and evaluate its potential for success by asking questions like these: "What have I built into the training to involve the student?" "How am I measuring the student's learning and the quality of my materials?" "How am I making the best use of the medium and of the student's time?" A computer-based program can ensure that every ten minutes of education is outstanding because the student must learn the lessons to continue. All the cost advantages of self-study are achieved with computer-based training. Of course, there is the cost of a personal computer to consider. If the equipment is used for five years, though, the cost amounts to a few dollars a day, a small price to pay for the tremendous increase in learning.

Everyone agrees that a personal tutor is the most effective teaching method, but who can afford a human tutor? On the other hand, a personal computer is an affordable tutor. This is the big breakthrough in education today.

The time and cost involved in developing a computer-based course are greater than for a classroom-based course or a self-study course that does not use computers, but this investment in effort and time raises the course quality. A computer-based course usually takes less time to teach than a classroom course, so the development costs are justifiable. Many of the education development companies discussed in Chapter 2 are developing such courses. They can spread their costs over hundreds or thousands of students, so the cost to develop a course can be as low as $20 or $30 per student. And you must remember that no matter what the cost of developing a course, this cost is a *one-time* charge. The cost of delivering a course is incremental for each student trained, and individualized learning is a key approach for containing those incremental costs.

INTERACTIVE VIDEODISC/PERSONAL COMPUTER

Some courses, including courses in management training, sales, instructor training, service (repair) training, communication skills, manufacturing training, and administrative training, are greatly enhanced by the use of video. Providing role models is important in the successful training of managers, sales personnel, and instructors. Compared to reading a book or listening to a lecture, actually seeing and hearing how a role should (and should not) be performed is a very powerful learning experience. Simulations of performing a task or repairing equipment are equally powerful. And when video is combined with a personal computer, another major breakthrough in the personal tutoring concept emerges: the interactive videodisc.

Everyone talks about the expense of interactive videodiscs and personal computers, but in reality the hardware costs only about $5 a day more, per student, than the cost of that same student's books. The cost to develop an interactive videodisc course may run to several hundred thousand dollars, but, if thousands of students take the course, the average cost per student is reasonable. Education companies such as Applied Learning, Spectrum-Interactive, Forum Corporation, Universal Training, Agora, Arthur Andersen & Co., SRA, Courseware, National Education Company, Wilson Learning, and others are investing millions of dollars in developing courses for this new personal tutoring system. As a result, several thousand courses already exist for teaching basic knowledge and job skills.

IMPACT OF INDIVIDUALIZED LEARNING

What does all this individualized learning mean to business? For IBM, moving thousands of student days out of classrooms into self-study or computer-based training means a savings in excess of $200 million each year. The enormous potential savings have led IBM to move more than 50 percent of its education in marketing and service to individualized learning centers in branch offices. Cost containment programs can, and are, saving organizations millions of dollars each year.

What do students say about individualized learning? Frankly, they often prefer going to an education center in Florida or California, especially in January, but do they learn as much or more with individualized learning? Yes, they do.

NEED FOR CLASSROOM EDUCATION

A need for classroom education will always exist. Only in the classroom can you see, hear, and interact with master teachers, executives, or expert speakers. Discussion of case studies and laboratory exercises also requires a classroom environment. The key to a cost-containment strategy is to distribute instruction between various cost-effective and educationally appropriate delivery systems.

The Advanced Technology Classroom

IBM has constructed major central education centers that demonstrate to employees that their education and development is important to the company. Students understand that while prerequisites—the basic facts and concepts—will be learned at personal computers in their local learning centers, their advanced courses will be taken at a central education center. IBM has invested several years of effort in developing the Advanced Technology Classroom, with the following objectives in mind:

1. To improve the quality of classroom education by requiring the use of the same instructional design techniques that are used in self-study and computer-based training.
2. To increase the interaction between instructors and students by borrowing techniques used in computer-based training. Questions are asked every ten minutes, and every student is constantly called on to make decisions and to be involved in the learning.
3. To increase the amount of learning and retention of the lessons.

Many educators' first impression of the Advanced Technology Classroom is that only IBM or an organization with similarly vast resources could afford the cost of such technology. Actually the technology employed adds only 2 to 4 percent to the overall facility cost. Given that learning increases by 20 to 40 percent in such facilities, the cost is easily justified.

The Advanced Technology Classroom provides each student with a keypad connected to a personal computer. The computer displays the class's responses and even compares this class to previous classes, allowing the instructor to immediately relate why some responses are not as good as others. The personal computer also enables the instructor to prepare a seamless presentation using computer graphics, slides, videotapes, audiotapes, and videodiscs. This added advantage permits more subjects to be covered in a shorter time, which is an obvious cost savings. The real breakthrough, however, is in the quality of education delivered by the Advanced Technology Classroom.

The satellite classroom system

There is another classroom delivery system in use today that is responsible for a breakthrough in education. This is the satellite communications classroom system. In the satellite framework, master teachers work either alone in a studio that looks like an evening news anchor desk or in a spontaneous, interactive classroom with a small group of students. Instruction is communicated by satellite to classrooms around the country. This is not an inexpensive system. In fact, a multimillion-dollar investment is required for an interactive satellite classroom system. You may have heard of satellite systems that were not successful. These one-way, low-cost systems were really communication, not education, systems. The system must be interactive to be an effective education delivery system. Students must be able to ask the teacher questions. The teacher must be able to ask students questions and immediately provide feedback for their answers and to reinforce certain lessons where necessary. As with any other delivery system, every ten minutes must be outstanding in an interactive satellite system.

Only very large organizations will be able to invest in satellite systems. IBM's satellite systems cover 20 major metropolitan areas and 23 plant sites. Over 200,000 student days are taught each year to both customers and IBM employees.

But where are the savings in a satellite system? First, the elimination of travel and living expenses for the students results in the saving of an enormous amount of money. Second, because the need to build multiple central education centers is eliminated, millions of dollars can be saved. And each master teacher can reach 50, 100, 150, or 200 students at once, so there is a reduction in the cost of instruction.

SETTING STANDARDS AND TRENDS TOWARD INDIVIDUALIZED LEARNING

As more and more technology is implemented, setting standards for equipment and networks becomes essential. Every instructor cannot use a different type of personal computer. Students should not be confused by different software programs. Multiple satellite networks would be prohibitively expensive. Standards are as essential to education as they are to management information systems.

There are two basic methods of delivering education: classroom instruction and individualized learning. In the 1970s, IBM used 75 percent classroom instruction and 25 percent individualized learning. By the end of the 1980s, these percentages will be 50-50. I predict that, by the end of the 1990s, the balance will have shifted to 25 percent classroom and 75 percent individualized learning. Years ago, no one would have predicted that a majority of employee training could be moved from the traditional classroom environment to the individualized learning center environment. This change signals a real revolution in education. Most educators still cannot believe that it is possible. Not only is it possible, but it is happening in a company that is often cited as the leader in employee education.

Why has this revolution occurred? Essentially, economics drives courses from the classroom to the individualized learning method. The growing desire to increase the quality of education has been an equally important driving force. If an organization converts a majority of its education program to alternative delivery systems, a dramatic increase in quality will follow.

TWO WAYS TO WASTE EDUCATION DOLLARS

Two major pitfalls are to be avoided if education funds are not to be wasted. First, you must be careful not to set an arbitrary number of days or hours for training. For example, do not require that all technical employees (engineers, programmers, scientists, etc.) have 48 hours of training per year. If your company employs 20,000 technical personnel, this decision will cost the company $18 million even if all the training is performed in a local education center. If 50 percent of that training occurs at a central education center, the cost of the 48-hour decision would be driven up to $30 million.

The cost of arbitrary decisions is impressive. Arbitrary decisions can occasionally force an improvement in the quality of education, but chances that this will happen are not good. It is much more likely that if 48 hours of training are arbitrarily required, part of the 48 hours will be "filler" to ensure that everyone has the required 48 hours of training.

Second, avoid the decision to spend 1, 2, or 10 percent of revenues—or any fixed percentage—on educating employees. Such a decision could lead to a waste of valuable resources or could result in insufficient training. The question, "How much should we spend on education?" has only one answer: "Spend what is required." Education is not like research. It is not an arbitrary expense. Education is an investment that provides a return in the form of the well-trained employees essential to an organization's performance.

SUMMARY

Unfortunately, thousands of employees go to work every day without the basic job training they require. Most companies are weak in employee training and development. The results of insufficient education programs are poor quality, errors, waste, loss of market share, poor customer service, and increased labor cost for additional employees. High attrition rates are often due to poor performance resulting from a lack of training. Employees who perform poorly lose their motivation and quit. It's too bad that our cost-accounting systems do not record problems like these.

All intermediate and large organizations should have multimillion-dollar budgets to train their employees. As organizations invest in adequate employee training, however, the need for workable cost-, containment programs will grow.

The other major challenge within education today is to raise the quality of education. That is the subject of the next chapter.

5 ///

How to Raise the Quality of Education

The question about how to raise the quality of education is constantly asked at board of education meetings, education conferences, and in the executive offices of corporations. More often than not, the traditional answers amount to "spend more money." The following measures are often suggested:

- Raise teachers' starting salaries to attract better people to careers in education.
- Pay experienced teachers more money to keep outstanding performers in education.
- Provide better facilities and working conditions to help people perform effectively.
- Reduce the average number of students in the classroom to allow more individual instruction and attention.
- Buy computers for every classroom.
- Hire more administrators, counselors, and other support personnel.

If spending more money were the answer, quality would be much higher today. You may be surprised, or appalled, to learn that in the 1980s, 16 percent of all college freshmen are enrolled in remedial reading courses, 21 percent in remedial writing, and 25 percent in remedial mathematics.

This chapter will discuss seven elements that are essential in raising the quality of education:

1. A new method of learning
2. A new, structured method for course development
3. High quality courses from education companies
4. New career paths for educators
5. New development programs for educators
6. New courses for future educators
7. A quality review system

The discussion begins by focusing on one of the most exciting methods to improve learning and retention—the interactive method of learning.

A NEW METHOD OF LEARNING

The point was made earlier that a manufacturing company would quickly go out of business if it could be proud of only the top 25 percent of its output. Yet, the fact that three-quarters of students who graduate from most educational institutions are *not* outstanding, but range from moderately prepared to utterly unprepared, is too often considered normal. Corporate directors of education cannot tolerate this level of performance, nor should the administrators of other educational institutions. Of course, major differences separate public schools and employee-training programs. For example:

- Students in public schools are not salaried, while in corporations employee-students are paid, on average, $25,000 to $40,000 per year. The cost of their salaries and benefits makes classroom time away from their jobs very expensive.
- Corporate education cannot accommodate failures or poor performers. No organization can afford poor performers when labor and benefits costs are as high as they are today.
- Employee training must motivate students to learn. An unmotivated employee is too expensive to tolerate.
- The lessons delivered by employee-training programs must be applied to the job or the money spent on training has been wasted.

These factors have motivated directors of employee training constantly to ask, "Are the students learning the lessons and retaining the knowledge?" This concern has created the need to develop various approaches to interactive learning that include frequent measurements of learning.

Computer-based training is an ideal example of interactive teaching. The computer demands constant student involvement. Every ten or fifteen minutes, the computer asks the student questions about the lessons learned during the past several minutes. If the student answers the questions correctly, the computer gives a positive motivational response and continues to the next information module or chapter. If the student doesn't answer the questions correctly, the computer gives an encouraging response and takes the student through some remedial training. In a few minutes, a new set of questions is asked to see if the student has now mastered the lesson.

The student feels no threat from the computer. The computer is extremely patient. It never gets irritated, mad, disgusted, annoyed, or upset with the student. The student and the computer work together to learn. Peer pressure is eliminated and the process of learning is enhanced. The student appreciates the privacy of learning without the threat of a "final test" or the aggravation that results from constantly being compared to other students. The personal computer as the personal tutor in the education process is one of the keys to a breakthrough in education.

In a well-designed computer-based course, the student knows that all the information in the course is important and must be mastered. The student also knows that he or she must learn each lesson before the computer will proceed to the next. The student cannot "fake it" or bluff his or her way through. All this motivates the student to learn.

As discussed in the previous chapter, some organizations are using satellite systems to allow a master teacher to reach several hundred students. If one-way video is used with no student response system, the students can be expected to pay about as much attention to the lesson as they do to a dull TV program at home. On the other hand, if an interactive system is used, the master teacher can engage in a two-way dialogue and ask questions, and all students must pay close attention. The master teacher must involve students constantly and "make every ten minutes outstanding." Their keypads allow students to answer multiple-choice questions, and the computer immediately tells the students how many correct answers were received and whether their individual answers were correct. The teacher in the central classroom can use this information to reinforce correct answers and provide any remedial instruction that seems necessary. When interactive student-response systems are used, the retention level has been proven to be as much as 20 percent greater than for the ordinary lecture method. Classrooms, too, can be made interactive with keypads. The Advanced Technology Classroom described in Chapter 4 uses interactive keypads. Of course, teachers can use questioning techniques in traditional classrooms to force participation, but too often this is not done.

The new methods to ensure that lessons are being learned must be complemented by new course-development methods to make certain that the right lessons are being taught. In other words, the content of courses must be improved. The second method for improving the quality of education is a systematic approach to course development.

A NEW, STRUCTURED METHOD FOR COURSE DEVELOPMENT

In the past, a course usually centered on a textbook written by an author who knew the subject. The book was professionally edited by a publishing company. Teachers using the book would build lesson plans from a course outline based on the text. Some teachers started with the first chapter and proceeded to the end of the book. Other teachers jumped around in the book because they felt they knew more than the author about the sequence in which the topics should be taught. Everyone remembers those teachers who were never able to cover all the material. I recall one high-school algebra teacher who covered only 60 pages in 18 weeks while others covered 200 to 300 pages. Needless to say, some of us were a little behind when we were promoted to the advanced algebra course.

Not long ago, employee-training courses were developed by instructors during periods when they were not teaching. Most of the instructors had no formal training in course development, creativity, writing, or other essential skills. This often resulted in courses that were much longer than necessary, not to mention poorly focused and not geared to the target audience as well as they might have been. Today, this method of part-time course development is being replaced by a system in which people who have had in-depth training in developing efficient, effective, and motivational courses are hired as full-time course developers. The large-volume courses offered in employee education today are sometimes designed by teams of professionals whose specialties include project management, subject-matter to-be-taught, instructional design, technical writing, measurement and evaluation, computer programming (if computers are involved), and media (print, audio, video, etc.). The one job on this list that may need explanation is that of the *instructional designer*. Instructional design is defined as the systematic approach to determining what an employee must know and be able to do to perform successfully in a major job category. The design of the instruction should include the use of cost-effective delivery systems and measurements to ensure that lessons will be learned, retained, and applied.

Instructional designers are educators with advanced degrees and are the experts on course design. Some people call them the "architects" of course development. They are responsible for the overall development, documentation, and evaluation of course materials. Their responsibilities also extend to the design of a curriculum in which a series of courses are integrated. Instructional designers are as important to the success of an education program as are the instructors. In fact, the instructional designers who build a high-volume classroom course are slightly more important to the course's success than are the ten instructors who actually administer the course lessons. With this much talent and expense being invested, there is a need for a highly structured course-development process. This process includes six phases:

1. *Analysis* of subject to be taught
2. *Design* of the course
3. *Developing* or writing the course
4. *Production* of various media
5. *Implementation* of pilot and ongoing classes
6. *Evaluation* of course content and student learning

The following sections treat each of these phases in detail.

Phase 1: Analysis of the subject to be taught

The first step in a systematic course development process is to gather and analyze the data that identifies exactly what knowledge and tasks must be taught. Sometimes, inexperienced course developers skip this step and begin by writing the course content that they feel should be included. Inevitably, problems arise. If the need for the course is not clearly defined, the right content areas may not be covered and students will discover that the lessons are not really relevant to the job that must be done. Inappropriate teaching techniques may be selected. Once again, an expensive, "nice to do" course is created rather than the essential, "need to know" course that is required to perform a job.

Both task analysis and topic analysis are necessary to define what students must learn to fill the gap between what they know and can do prior to the course and what they must know and be able to do after completing the course.

Phase 2: Design of the course

The instructional designers, who were part of the analysis phase, perform a "color rendering" and lay out the "blueprints" of a course before course construction starts. The first step of course design is to write a course's learning objectives, also known as "content objectives". These statements define the desired knowledge or performance skills to be learned. Students should be informed of the learning objectives before the course begins to let them know what is expected of them and to enable them to judge their own success. Knowing the objectives gives students a sense of control and involves them in taking responsibility for their own learning.

Then, the instructional designers will list in great detail the course's "teaching points," that is, the key messages that the course must deliver to the student. In a five-day course, there may be several hundred teaching points.

In the next step, the designers decide on the process that will be employed to teach the key messages. Examples of teaching processes include the following:

- Readings
- Lectures
- Case studies
- Demonstrations
- Hands-on exercises
- Role playing
- Tests
- Job aids
- Simulations

The intent of the overall design is to make every ten minutes outstanding, so that the student will maintain interest in the subject. To enable students to learn in a logical manner, the instructional designer must carefully sequence the teaching points so that they are presented according to a logical flow.

Finally, the instructional designer must decide on the delivery system to be used, which might be classroom, computer-based training, or self-study. Within any delivery system strategy, many decisions must be made about the use of various media, such as

- Flip charts (sometimes called easel charts)
- Chalk boards
- Foils and transparencies
- Slides
- Handouts
- Videotapes and films
- Videodiscs
- Personal computers
- Student workbooks
- Instructor guides

Education experts report that adults have different requirements for effective instruction than do children. Good instructional designers focus on the following principles of adult learning:

1. *Problem-centered versus subject-centered approach.* In teaching adults, the focus should be on current, existing problems rather than abstract concepts, emphasizing the "need to know" rather than the "nice to know." Problem-solving techniques should be targeted.

2. *Immediate application.* Knowledge and skills should be provided that can be used immediately to resolve real-world problems that appear on a day-to-day basis. Exercises should let learners practice and apply new knowledge and skills within the education event—before they go on to use them on the job.

3. *Building on previous experience.* The vast array of experience that an adult audience brings to a learning environment should be acknowledged. Incorporating this knowledge and experience into a course widens the scope of learning for other participants.

4. *Learner control.* The learner should have maximum control over the learning process, based on what is needed on the job. This means that the instructor should serve as a facilitator rather than a content specialist. Options should be provided to meet individual needs and interests.

5. *Active participation.* Adults need to be actively involved in the learning process so that they learn by doing. The integration of what is learned can be maximized by structuring activities to incorporate seeing, hearing, talking, and doing.

6. *Whole-part-whole sequencing.* The course structure should present the overview (or "big picture"), move on to the details, and then return to the whole in order to integrate and relate the parts within it.

7. *Association.* Using previous experiences will help learners associate material learned in the past with new situations. By relating the new and the old, the course can enable students to build on known information and skills.

8. *Integrative, wholistic thinking.* The analytic skills used to make deductions and explore details can be developed through exercises such as situation analyses. Training in analytic skills needs to be complemented by exercises (such as brain teasers) that develop students' intuitive abilities—the skills that enable them to make inductions and explore whole pictures.

9. *Individual learning rates and styles.* Adults learn at different rates and in different ways, so a variety of instructional techniques to accommodate these differences should be provided.

10. *Time spent completing tasks.* Tutorials should be designed to last no longer than 10 to 15 minutes before moving on to practice and application of the skills and knowledge taught in the tutorial.

11. *Meaningful instructional cues.* A clear explanation of what is to be learned, the expected outcomes, and evaluation criteria should be given. Learners need to be provided with tests, exercises, and other cues to determine when they have reached competency.

12. *Checking for understanding.* Frequent checks will ensure that students are understanding the material and making progress. Remediation aids and reinforcement activities will further ensure comprehension and retention.

13. *Feedback.* Consistent information should be provided to let learners know how well they are progressing. Success should be rewarded with credit and recognition, and remedial techniques and exercises should be designed for those times when students fail to learn the lessons. It is important to fully explain to the learner why he or she is either right or wrong.

The evaluation strategy must also be defined in this phase (you will learn about this in the sixth phase of course development, below).

Phase 3: Developing or writing the course

If a thorough job has been done in the analysis and design phases, the writing of the course will proceed on schedule. Unfortunately, all of the shortcuts taken and all of the work left undone during the analysis and design phases must be completed in this phase. For this reason, some projects go off schedule in the development phase.

Although some instructional designers write their own scripts and books, professional writers or course authors often enter the picture at this phase of course development. They take the learning objectives, teaching points, and all of the course design documentation and begin to write the course materials. During this phase of the project, the course authors will confer frequently with subject-matter experts and instructional designers.

At some point, a course author may begin to feel that he or she knows better than the instructional designer how to design the course. And frequently the instructional designer will try to tell the course author how to write the course. It is this "artistic" conflict of opinions that makes the development phase interesting. In reality, you need the best thinking of both the instructional designers and the course authors to have a successful project. The project manager must manage these artistic differences of opinions.

At the completion of the development phase a validation test, using potential students, must be performed. The validation test uses draft materials to help decide if the students have learned what is required to achieve the course objectives. After the validation test and prior to the production phase of course development, there is a period of fine-tuning of the course materials. This period of rewriting is crucial, so it must be scheduled properly so that the project does not go off schedule before production has even started.

Phase 4: Production of various media

By the time the production phase is reached the course materials have been written and tested on students. Now, the validated and fined-tuned drafts must be converted into various media, including

- Print materials (such as students' materials, instructors' guides, measurement tools, exercises, etc.)
- Overhead transparencies (foils)

- Slides
- Videotapes and films
- Videodiscs
- Computer programs, perhaps including programs that merge with videodiscs

At this time, the subject-matter experts and instructional designers review all of the production work in great detail. This review is not intended to bring up new ideas and "improvements" for the course, but rather to be sure the course is being produced faithfully according to the specifications of the design documents. This is the production, or construction, phase, and major changes mean substantial increases in cost. This is a hectic time, and the project management system is usually challenged to its limits. Again, the project manager must maintain control of essential changes.

Phase 5: Implementation of pilot and ongoing classes

When all the course materials have been produced, the moment to implement the course will finally arrive. A pilot group or two often provides a safe way to launch a new course, whether it is a classroom or an individualized learning course. The course developers and subject-matter experts quite often serve as instructors in pilot classes. After all, who else is better qualified to teach a course than its inventors? On the other hand, many companies prefer that well-prepared teachers instruct the first class, with the subject matter-experts and instructional designers on hand for advice and counsel.

The pilot group will sometimes have fewer students than would a regular class, which permits time to debrief the students carefully about the effectiveness of the course. The selection of students must not bias the results by using above-average students, but rather should be as representative as possible of the target population. One method of selection is to choose people from various departments, functions, and geographic locations to participate.

For courses that will be delivered in a classroom environment, "teach the teacher" classes usually follow pilot classes. In these teacher classes it is a big mistake not to allow the new instructors sufficient time to interact with the course developers and subject-matter experts. One method of ensuring success is to set aside twice the time for a "teach the teacher" class as for a normal class. Teach during the first half of the day and then review in great detail the course materials and design during the second half of the day.

Most successful courses include a followup system so that course developers can see how successful the courses are. This leads to the final phase of course development, which is course evaluation.

Phase 6: Evaluation of the course content and student learning

The final step in the course development process is to evaluate the information collected from early groups taking the course. In the design phase of the process, the instructional designers develop an evaluation strategy for the course. Four essential levels of evaluation should be used to obtain results. Table 4 shows the four levels, the key question each answers, and some recommended ways to measure the effectiveness of the course.

Many training departments within corporations and not-for-profit organizations try to avoid measurements. They want to assume that if people attend class, they learn. But if you want to command

Table 4. Levels of Evaluation

Level	Key Question	Methods of Measuring
1. Reactions	Did the students react favorably to the course?	• Questionnaires • Interviews
2. Knowledge/Skill	Did the students improve their knowledge and skill as a result of the course?	• Before and after tests • Observations • Performance problems • Simulations
3. Application	Are the students able to apply what they learned to improve their job performance?	• Tests or observations on the job, or under joblike conditions • Performance records • Surveys of managers
4. Business Results	Did the results of the course have a favorable impact on business performance?	• Performance records • Cost analysis

adequate resources and respect for education programs you must have a comprehensive and appropriate set of measurements. Corporate education programs are beginning to integrate measurement systems so that the value of the resources being invested in job training and employee education can be clearly demonstrated.

Many instructors and course developers ask the question, "Do we really have to use such a highly structured course development process?" Too often, they are ready to take shortcuts, which often result in the course being redeveloped several times over its life. Unfortunately, unlike manufacturing organizations, education departments do not have cost-accounting systems to record "scrap" and work performed all over again. But education wastes millions of dollars on scrap and "re-work" every year. The other cost associated with low quality in course development comes from the remedial training and followup course work that are required when the first effort is not on target.

Earlier in this chapter, it was stated that, for many years, instructors were asked to create courses in their spare time or when they were not teaching. Because instructors were not trained in structured course design, those courses were usually 25 to 40 percent longer than was necessary, which raised the expense of employee education. Companies have learned that a structured course-development process like the one just described often results in more effective education at less expense. The team of course development professionals will typically pay for itself by building courses in which students learn more information more effectively and in a shorter period of time.

PURCHASE HIGH-QUALITY COURSES FROM EDUCATION COMPANIES

Many large organizations are using education course development companies to create their large-volume courses. These education companies have professional teams of project managers, instructional designers, course authors, media specialists, computer programmers, and testing experts. The contracting companies provide the subject-matter experts, and the education companies develop the courses.

The quality of these courses is outstanding compared to many courses taught in the average company, public school, or university. Lessons are often taught in a fraction of the time required by teachers in traditional systems. Sometimes a company will spend $250,000 to $500,000 to develop a five-day course: a significant investment that will save millions in the cost of delivery by reducing the time spent in a conventional lecture hall. Justifying the expense of such course development requires that measurement systems be in place to ensure that students learn the lessons and apply them to their jobs.

Three fundamental questions can be used as a guide for managing projects undertaken with course-development companies:

1. Does the course that the course-development company produces achieve the applicable quality measurements?
2. Is the project completed on time?
3. Did the project remain within budget?

Education companies face stiff competition. Either their performance is outstanding or they go out of business. Many not only do custom course-development for large employee education organizations but offer high quality "off-the-shelf" courses. Some companies have several hundred such courses, and a few offer several thousand. Almost every corporation today buys or rents courses from education course-development companies, which are also leaders in the application of cost-effective delivery systems.

NEW CAREER PATHS FOR EDUCATORS

Years ago, I was the IBM account executive for one of the world's largest merchandising companies. We were engaged in converting millions of credit accounts to the computer. One day, in a meeting with the vice president of credit and his key executives to review how the application would be programmed for the computer, one executive asked, "What will we do with the two programmers once the credit job is implemented on the computer?" I tried to explain that they would always need some computer programmers to maintain the programs and to modify them, for instance, when the rate of interest changed. The situation was a difficult one because, back then, programmers were thought to be a special breed, whose services would only be required on a temporary basis. It was hard for executives to understand that these people would be part of the credit department on a long-term basis. I would guess that, today, this organization has at least 50 programmers in its credit department. The employees who designed and programmed the initial credit application have become the experts on the internal procedures of the increasingly complex credit application.

The same situation exists in education today. Except for the position of instructor, all jobs are considered temporary. Instructional designers, media personnel, education technology experts, and others are rarely on career paths within large education departments. But this is beginning to change. To develop—and benefit from—such career paths, a company must be able to

- Attract individuals with high potential
- Develop outstanding people
- Retain selected outstanding people
- Place successful instructors and developers in positions of great responsibility

For an individual employee, career positions define an area of potential growth within an organization. The positions provide a structure around which the employee can track his or her personal growth plans and around which the manager can establish development plans to assure growth in and beyond the present position. With a defined career path, managers and employees can make good decisions regarding training, development, education, and future assignments. To put it simply, a defined career path represents *opportunity*. Conversely, an ill-defined or nonexistent career path represents little or no opportunity.

In the past, education or training departments within corporations, government agencies, and not-for-profit organizations have not often been regarded as places in which to "move ahead." Several reasons can be cited for this view:

- The general image of education as outside the mainstream of the business
- The perception of education positions as either transient or dead-end from the career viewpoint
- The lack of a clear view of education's magnitude and its importance to the organization's success

As a result of these impressions, four broad categories of individuals are often found working in education departments. First, there is a small group of dedicated people who have found education to be a fulfilling and challenging career even though a formal development path has not existed. Second, there is the person on rotational assignment, for whom the focus of the assignment is a development experience en route to a position of greater responsibility. Third, there

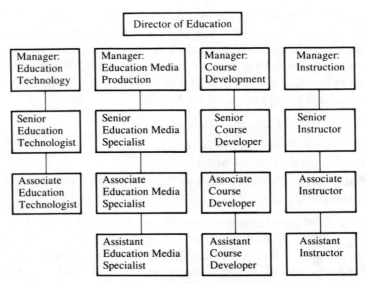

FIGURE 2. Positions in an education department.

is the solid but unimpressive performer who remains in the education department because the manager finds it difficult to place him or her in a job of greater responsibility. Finally, there is that small group of people who were hired because they have professional training in teaching and/or course development. Members of this last group are sometimes referred to as "professional hires."

The professional educators who have built the existing courses and programs in most organizations probably comprise too small a group to deal with the explosive growth that will occur in the 1990s and beyond. There is a real need to develop many outstanding educators who will have long careers both as instructors and course developers. Figure 2 shows the specific positions within an education department, each of which has a distinct set of competencies associated with it. The illustration is not intended to imply that every education department will have all of these positions, but rather to show the number of opportunities that may exist in the future. The basic job categories shown in the figure can be defined as follows:

- *Instructor.* Responsible for the delivery of courses designed for classroom use as well as for other activities, including course maintenance, some course development for unique site or function requirements, student liaison, class management, and coordination of visiting speakers

- *Course developer.* Responsible for application of instructional design principles to development of courses, particularly those intended for broad use within the company, those that use a self-study approach, and those incorporating such advanced delivery systems as computer-based training, interactive video, and advanced, multimedia classrooms
- *Education media specialist.* Responsible for production of effective education media deliverables, particularly in courses using technologically advanced delivery systems
- *Education technologist.* Responsible for application of a broad range of skills supporting the advancement of education technology in the company's education

Because education plays a critical role in helping each major area of a business meet strategic and tactical objectives, the education department is challenged to maintain a high level of staff competency and vitality as the pace of change quickens and the organization's dynamics become more complex. A key to implementing career paths is sound staff selection. An effective staffing foundation selects the most qualified candidates for education, enables them to become effective and productive as quickly as possible, and then places them into challenging assignments. This leads to the next subject: how to improve the quality of education for educators.

NEW DEVELOPMENT PROGRAMS FOR EDUCATORS

Almost every organization has some type of instructor training and development program, usually lasting from two to five days. The program tells a new instructor how to have good eye contact, how to use visual aids, how to ask questions, and other basic facts about teaching. This may seem short and inadequate, but remember, this is usually more training than is provided for inexperienced, first-year instructors at universities.

Unfortunately, the fact that instructors in most organizations do not have adequate training means that most beginning instructors believe that they should use the lecture method: that is, stand up and tell the students what they, as teachers, know. Actually, the instructor's role is to close the gap between what students know when they enter the course and the skills and knowledge that those students must possess to perform the job for which they are being trained. The instructor's role should therefore be defined primarily as a *change agent and catalyst,* not solely as an information imparter.

Most new instructors bring to the job four basic qualities:

- *Positive attitude.* Instructors are pleased with the assignment and view it as an opportunity.
- *Subject matter expertise.* Instructors typically bring a high experience level to the subjects they are to teach. This gives them credibility and comfort.
- *Presentation skills.* Most instructors have good verbal skills, poise, and an ability to think well on their feet in front of others or they would never have considered working in an education department.
- *Good employee.* Instructors are good role models for those they teach, which is usually one reason they were selected to do the job.

New instructors need training for six major responsibilities:

- *Preparing to teach.* This activity is heaviest during the first few months of a new instructor's assignment. However, each time a class is scheduled, the instructor must prepare the lesson plans, the visuals, the facilities, and the instructional materials, and must perform a host of other tasks. Unless the instructor is properly trained, he or she may simply leap from crisis to crisis.
- *Teaching the class.* Instructional skills are of two types: platform skills and facilitating skills. New instructors are primarily concerned with platform skills and with putting information into students' heads. They tend to lecture and will do so forever if not trained to be effective facilitators. Facilitation requires training in asking questions, creating situations for learning, and giving students an opportunity to apply their new learning in class.
- *Designing and developing instructional materials.* Given the need to update, refine, expand, and tailor the materials that go with a course, instructors devote time and energy to keeping their courses current and even in developing new courses. The instructors require training in adult learning techniques, learning theory, course design, needs analysis, selection of media, writing, preparing case studies, role playing, simulation, and testing.
- *Evaluating learners' performance.* Instructors are responsible for keeping performance records, preparing written student evaluations, and giving constructive feedback. This is done periodically during the course, and not simply as an end-of-course exercise.

Too often, there is no training for these tasks and this important responsibility is neglected.

- *Advising students.* Instructors give advice and counsel when needed. This means applying directive and nondirective techniques of coaching and counseling, which requires some special training or there is that risk that students may lose motivation.
- *Transferring new learning.* Instructors should be concerned with student performance back on the job and not simply in class. This means using a variety of tools and techniques to maximize the transfer of training and to assure maintenance of new behavior in the workplace. The majority of instructors are never given any training in this responsibility, and this is why too many courses focus on the "nice to have" rather than the essentials for teaching an employee how to do a job.

Enhanced instructor training and development programs will almost always raise the quality of education in most organizations.

Unfortunately, full-time course developers rarely receive formal training because there are very few schools to train them. Most developers are not trained instructional designers, nor are they trained in writing, media selection, or other major responsibilities of their jobs. They usually learn on the job, and the results show that that is a hit-and-miss learning situation. This is why so many organizations are using outside education-development companies to create new courses. These companies have usually done an outstanding job of selecting and training their personnel. Their courses are usually superior to those developed in many organizations.

Some companies are finally investing in customized university programs to train course developers. These classes are not three-to-five-day-long affairs, but represent several weeks of intensive training. Such programs are a sound investment if you want to develop outstanding courses.

A few companies, and they are still very few, are training managers of education on a broad range of subjects, including

- Education-requirements planning
- Structured course-development processes
- Media production
- Instructor management
- Education-center operations
- Library and learning-center operations

- Education measurements
- Budgets and financial measurements
- Computer support programs for education
- Administrative planning and support
- People-management techniques
- Quality control programs
- Business planning

The performance of the education department influences the performance of the entire company. Many organizations are beginning to realize that the resources of their education departments require better management. Management training within the education departments is, therefore, a sound investment and has a multiplier effect.

Where will the new people come from to staff the growing education organizations? Normally, future instructors and course developers will come from within an organization, having demonstrated their talents as successful salespeople, programmers, engineers, and so on. Another source that could have a positive impact on the quality of education is to hire graduates from colleges of education.

NEW COURSES REQUIRED FOR FUTURE EDUCATORS

Many schools of education at major universities have been reduced in size and scope because of the decline in the need for primary and secondary school teachers. Too many schools of education are either not aware of or not concerned with preparing graduates to enter the new industrial education field. This is an unfortunate situation, because a shortage of instructional designers will occur if technology continues to move at its current pace in corporate education organizations. Employee education departments need graduates with professional educational training. There is an even greater need to change the courses and curricula at schools of education to meet the requirements of the industrial education departments. Here are some types of courses required to supplement traditional education programs:

- In-depth writing courses, which are often available in journalism schools or in fine arts departments and English departments (that is, in the school of liberal arts)
- Media courses, focusing on audio tapes, videotapes, videodiscs, graphics, slides, and film, and which are usually offered in a university's school of communications

- Basic business courses, such as accounting, finance, management, marketing, economics and personnel administration, which are offered in a university's business school
- Computer concepts and programming courses, which are usually offered in a university's computer science department (often a part of the school of engineering)
- Professional education courses, including course development, which are offered in a university's school of education

The problem is clear. To ask five or six existing colleges or departments within a university to cooperate on a new curriculum of courses is to ask for much more than most universities are willing to do. The challenge is even greater when there is no large company or foundation to make a multimillion-dollar grant of incremental funds to create such a curriculum. This *is* the curriculum of courses, however, that will provide college graduates with the knowledge and skills needed to enter industrial education departments directly. A real demand exists for students with this training, and if they are good performers, they will be on their way to well-paid careers in education and to great job satisfaction. The alternative is to continue with the existing situation, in which graduates of these various schools take another five to ten years to learn on the job. An instructional designer today normally requires at least five years of experience plus a master's or doctoral degree to be a qualified candidate to enter an industrial education department. As more people become aware of the good salaries, good job opportunities, and job satisfaction such companies provide, more universities will offer degrees in instructional design and industrial education.

IMPLEMENT A QUALITY REVIEW SYSTEM

Several companies have implemented small quality-control departments responsible for reviewing all new courses as well as for performing periodic reviews of existing large-volume courses. The intent of such reviews is to achieve an independent view regarding the following questions:

1. Does the course have sound business requirements and who are the executive sponsors of the course?
2. Has the audience for the course been well defined? What major jobs require this course? Where does the course fit into the existing curriculum?

3. Was a task analysis completed prior to the design of the course? What do the students need to know and do?
4. Have a needs analysis and a cost analysis been completed? Do the sponsoring executives agree to the cost to develop and deliver the course?
5. Are the learning objectives clearly stated?
6. Are the detailed teaching points documented and properly sequenced?
7. Did the course developers build in efficient, effective, and motivational methods of teaching?
8. Are the students challenged and exercised throughout the course to be certain they learn and retain the lessons?
9. What are the plans to determine whether the lessons are applied on the job?
10. Have all the drafts been completed for all media used in the course? What is the level of quality of the print materials? Are the visuals outstanding?
11. Has the teacher training session been well planned? Are there good teaching outlines?
12. Are we using the most cost-effective delivery systems?

Too many education departments let course developers and/or instructors evaluate their own courses. This is like letting the person in charge of the petty cash box audit the petty cash accounts.

SUMMARY

The vast majority of education measurements today focus on the quantity of education. Measuring quality has not been the top priority in most education organizations. Most companies do not know the total cost of their education programs; even fewer organizations have measured quality.

Measurements are the real key to improving quality. An organization must be able to determine where it is at present, to set goals for quality improvements, and to measure the performance of course developers and instructors until they reach the desired quality levels. This will happen when executives insist on more measurement and demand evidence of improved quality in return for their investments in education. There is no excuse for students not learning. Most students start schools or other educational programs wanting to be successful. If educational organizations decide that their goal is to train all students successfully, they will find methods to reach that goal. Change is required in

- how courses are designed and developed
- how lessons are taught
- how quality is measured

All of these changes are feasible today.

6 ///

Having the Right Person in the Right Course

The glamorous jobs in education today involve working with new delivery systems, such as computer-based training, videodiscs, and satellites. Not only is it interesting to work with these new methods of communicating lessons, but they usually provide the most effective way to show a breakthrough in the cost of education. At this point, most organizations are at least investigating the use of new, cost-effective delivery systems.

Another major cost breakthrough will occur when we can guarantee that the right person is in the right course at the right time. To do this sounds easy, but too often we are educating the wrong person at the wrong time in the wrong class. This unfortunate situation is one of the greatest challenges facing directors of education. Most of us who have managed large education organizations have struggled with this challenge, and most of us have more failures than successes to show for our efforts. To choose an example from my own history, I was a requirements manager for the marketing division of IBM during the mid-1970s, and I inherited a typical requirements process. My department sent a survey to the product marketing departments, the industry (applications) marketing departments, and to line management asking, "How much education do you want next year?" Each year, the answer was always at least 30 percent more than I could possibly deliver. Some years, it was 50 percent more.

Why not? If you were in charge of a product, wouldn't you request a week of education for every marketing representative, every systems engineer, and for the thousands of customers? I would. Product managers know that sales and installations are highly dependent upon knowledge.

This requirements process included the annual ritual of the "in plan" and "out plan." The "in plan" said that, with current resources (headcount and budget), I could provide this much education. My constant plea to the financial people was, "Give me more resources and I will provide more education from the 'out plan.'" The financial people would reply, "If we give you the millions you are requesting, we will need to raise prices by at least 5 percent." Inevitably, when I told the product managers that we might need a price increase to pay for the education they had requested, they would say, "Forget all that education we asked for in the "out plan."

The net result from these experiences was that I developed an uncomfortable feeling about the entire requirements process. Maybe this feeling originates in my accounting background. In accounting, two plus two must always equal four, and debits have to equal credits. In education requirements, the numbers never seemed to add up to satisfied customers. Needless to say, I was determined to find a solution to the problems inherent in the requirements process. Here is my latest thinking on this important subject.

FORGING A PARTNERSHIP

First, the education department must have a formal working partnership with the corporate functional staffs and line management so that it understands the business strategies and requirements needed to meet current goals. At IBM, that means that once a year the vice presidents of marketing, service, product development (engineering), software development, manufacturing, information systems, personnel, and finance present their strategic plans to the education management team. The annual meeting is a one-day event. The directors of education for each functional area are also expected to attend the key staff meetings of the functional vice presidents. For example, the director of service education must have a continuous working relationship with the management team of the service organization, which includes participation in their staff meetings. This process was not easy to establish, but once the functional vice presidents realized that the productivity of their employees was highly dependent on the training programs they received, the vice presidents all agreed to set up this partnership with the education departments.

FROM BUSINESS REQUIREMENTS TO EDUCATION REQUIREMENTS

The next important step is for the education department to translate business requirements into performance requirements, that is, what employees must know and be able to do. Only after the education department has translated business into performance requirements can the true education requirements be determined.

Again, all this sounds simple, but 95 percent of the Fortune 500 companies would fail an audit on translating business requirements to performance requirements to education requirements. It is a difficult process, so difficult, in fact, that many organizations give up, claiming, "This does not apply to our organization; we are different."

However, *not* doing this translation provides another reason for viewing education as an expense. As was stated before, most line executives spend only a few minutes on education each year. The one meeting is usually scheduled to approve the education budget. Within the traditional approach to defining requirements, education departments are always asking for an increase in resources to meet the so-called demand for education. If the organization is having a good year, executive management will usually agree to a good increase for education, which is typically somewhere between 5 and 15 percent. If business results for a given year are poor, the education budget usually gets cut by 5 to 10 percent.

Executives cannot understand the need for millions of dollars to support thousands (or millions) of student days. The question with which they understandably respond to most education presentations is, "What damage would be done if we cut the education budget request by 20 percent?" Executives are not negative about education; they simply have not been told what they will get in return for investing those huge sums of money. The relationship between business requirements (with which they are familiar) and education requirements (with which they are probably not familiar) has not been made clear.

EDUCATION AS AN INVESTMENT

It cannot be stated forcefully enough that the key to managing education lies in having the executive management team view education as an investment. "You give me so much headcount and dollars, and I will return to you so many trained employees." An investment implies a significant, measurable return on the personnel and money invested. The return on an education investment must be well-trained and more productive employees.

To be successful, organizations must invest in buildings, product development, manufacturing processes, advertising, marketing, service, *and* employee training. Too often, we see organizations invest in beautiful buildings, great merchandise, and superb advertising and then fail to invest in the employee training to support all that other investment. Banks, retail stores, restaurants, and automobile dealerships too often provide classic examples of situations in which investments become meaningless because of the poor employee performance. The jobs have not been defined, employees are not trained, and no one supervises their performance.

Here are the two major reasons for investing in education and training programs:

1. To train employees to do their current jobs at a level that will ensure your organization meets or exceeds annual objectives
2. To educate the top performers to take on jobs of greater responsibility

If someone today wanted to enter the business of selling low-cost but quality hamburgers, he or she would be forced by industry competition to have an outstanding training program for employees and managers. Ray Kroc, the founder of McDonald's, dramatically changed the fast-food industry by building Hamburger University in a suburb of Chicago. He has opened thousands of his golden-arched restaurants around the world. Millions of customers patronize them because they know the establishments will be clean, well run, and efficient, and that the food will be of consistent quality. A well-run restaurant requires training for each major job. No one could survive as a McDonald's competitor without training every employee and manager.

If you were to compare the largest 2,000 business, government, and not-for-profit organizations in the United States to McDonald's, you would find millions of employees and managers who have not been trained for their jobs to the same level as McDonald's employees and managers. Two major reasons are given for cheating on required training:

1. We do not have the time to train you because there is so much work to do. We simply cannot take you off the job to train you.
2. We do not have the budget to train you for your job, so just stand next to an experienced employee and learn from that person.

JUSTIFYING THE INVESTMENT

How do you justify the time and expense to train employees and managers? In most organizations, the answer is to make major changes in the requirements process. There are two fundamental ways to structure education requirements.

Defining requirements by major subject

The first method of structuring education is by major subject. This leads to the question, "What courses do you want?" The wish list is endless. If this method is used, an organization either will be frustrated because the education department can't meet the perceived demand or will have 50 to 100 percent more courses than are really required. An example will show how this method can bankrupt the education budget.

In the mid-1970s IBM determined that marketing representatives needed a firm grasp on four major subjects to sell large computer systems. The company therefore invested in the development of outstanding courses for the marketing representatives. A two-week course in Poughkeepsie, New York, covered the operating system products. In Raleigh, North Carolina, an equally good course covered the telecommunication products. San Jose, California, was the locale for the third two-week course, this one on database products. And the fourth course, addressing the integration of the products, was held in White Plains, New York. These courses constituted a major commitment, and the marketing education department insisted, "Outstanding education exists, and line management should force marketing representatives to take these courses." Line management answered, "We cannot afford that. The courses are too long and have too many duplicate lessons." By combining the four courses into a single two-week Large Systems Marketing Institute, the requirements of line management were met. The problem was solved and millions of dollars were saved because education was forced to take a job orientation to education requirements.

Defining requirements by major job

The second method and the recommended approach to education requirements is based on the major jobs within an organization. Very few organizations use this approach. It may come as a surprise to many readers that most companies have never identified a list of major jobs. It's a surprisingly difficult task. At IBM, it took almost two years to identify the 85 key jobs that covered more than 90 percent of its employees—a list that could be agreed upon and accepted by executive management, corporate functional staff executives, group and division line executives, and personnel. At various points during the compilation of this list, the list was narrowed to as few as 16 major jobs and then expanded to include as many as several thousand. I would constantly remind the education managers that job definitions had to support a curriculum of courses based on what they wanted each employee to know and do. We had to arrive at a manageable, but meaningful, number.

What are the advantages of designing requirements by major jobs?

1. This method identifies the voids in education programs. Most companies are shocked to find how many key jobs have almost no job training. Most executives believe everyone is being trained when they see the annual budget for education and training, but too often that is not the case.

2. Duplicate courses will be identified. Most organizations will discover they have too many courses for some jobs, such as sales training and management training. Sometimes the number of courses drops by 10 to 25 percent after curricula are designed for major jobs.

3. Allocating education headcount and budget on the basis of major job categories gives executives a way of clearly seeing the return they will receive on their investment. For the first time, the education director is able to say, "Give me this many personnel and this much money, and I will give you these trained employees in return."

4. This method permits executive management, corporate staff executives, line management, and education management to agree on four key issues:

- Who should be educated
- What courses should be taught
- When the courses should be offered
- What the required resources to accomplish the education and training mission are

Most executives have no problem in approving budget reductions if all they see is a savings in the number of student days, but they will find it much more difficult to slash the education budget if they see that the reduction will result in untrained employees.

With this new approach, discussions regarding the number of student days, student completions, days per salesperson, and so on become a thing of the past. Such discussions were never fully understood by executives because the old method of presenting requirements never communicated the return on investment. Executives were reviewing meaningless statistics in an effort to determine what level of expense was affordable.

Once major jobs are identified, the managers within the education organization should be identified as curriculum managers, each responsible for the tasks of developing curriculum specific to a particular job category, including

1. Determining the knowledge and skills required to do a job
2. Designing a curriculum of courses that permits employees to grow to various levels of capability, such as

   - Entry
   - Experienced
   - Expert

3. Tracking the number of employees at each level of capability and comparing it to the number that should be at that level (identifying this gap is how true education requirements are determined)

An organization needs a common enrollment and administrative system to feed course completions into a personnel database that maintains the education and training record for each employee. Too often, companies that do record course completions in personnel records end up with meaningless transcripts that no one understands or pays any attention to. If, however, a curriculum is defined by major jobs, each employee education record could be printed out once a year on a single, letter-size sheet that would clearly provide the following information:

- What entry training programs were completed?
- What jobs has the employee been trained on and to what level (entry, experienced, expert)?
- What advanced functional schools (education courses for employees identified for more responsible jobs) were completed?
- What management development courses were completed?
- What formal education does the employee have (high school, university)?

This one-page training and education record is important to a formal employee-development program. Once a year, a manager should sit down with each employee to discuss how he or she can stay current with the job, develop knowledge and skills, and become a competitive candidate for jobs of greater responsibility. Education planning for each employee is an important part of this process. It helps foster promotion from within and reduces costly employee attrition. This new education requirements process brings real meaning to career planning.

AN APPROACH TO CURRICULUM PLANNING

All this leads to the next logical question. How should an organization plan curricula once the major jobs are identified? The system for curriculum planning used in several companies is a basic, ten-step model and is performed in three phases.

Phase 1: needs analysis for an entire job

The purpose of the needs analysis phase is to identify those business needs that will be met by a series of courses within a curriculum. That curriculum will provide the knowledge and skills required to do one of the major jobs within an organization. In the needs analysis phase, there are three steps:

Step 1: Plan the analysis
Step 2: Collect the data
Step 3: Analyze the data

When this phase is completed the course designer will know

- The tasks employees need to do productive work
- The knowledge and skill requirements of each task
- What workers already know about the task

Phase 2: curriculum design

The curriculum design is a plan to maximize learning by relating two or more learning events to one another so that they form a coordinated unit in terms of content areas. Design includes definition of the learning objectives for both the whole curriculum and the individual courses, plus identification of the major teaching points to be delivered in each course. There are three steps within the curriculum design phase:

Step 4: Identify purposes and objectives
Step 5: Determine content and sequence
Step 6: Produce the curriculum design

The curriculum design is a document to guide the development of each specific course or learning event. It is also a planning document consulted in major reviews of the overall curriculum architecture before specific courses or learning events are developed or revised.

Phase 3: curriculum plan of action

The curriculum design will not be activated until a variety of decisions are made, implementation activities scheduled, persons assigned to take responsibility for their completion, and management agreement secured to provide personnel and funds to build the courses. Phase 3 is critical for curriculum implementation. It includes the following four steps:

Step 7: Estimate cost
Step 8: Establish priorities
Step 9: Schedule development tasks
Step 10: Create curriculum plans and obtain agreements

In Step 7, the total curriculum costs, including development and delivery, are estimated. These estimates are key to the justification decisions. With this information, the education department is in a position to make a compelling presentation to company executives. This presentation will provide the following information:

1. The number of employees within a major job who need to be trained to three levels (entry, experienced, expert)
2. The payroll and benefits cost of this group of employees
3. An explanation of how this group of employees doing this particular job involves the use of millions of dollars in buildings, utilities, equipment, and so on, and of how their performance

impacts areas of customer satisfaction, sales quotas, and/or vendor relations

4. An account of the cost of education and training to prepare these people to do their jobs, showing it to be a reasonable investment when the three factors above are considered

5. A demonstration of how, with this investment in education and training, the employees will process this knowledge (list the major lessons) and be able to perform these tasks (list the major tasks)

6. An explanation of how, without this investment in education, the number of employees would have to be 5, 10, or 15 percent greater (or more) to compensate for unstructured job training, remedial work, and increased errors

Executives can understand the value of education and training when the justification story is told this way. If a company has 25 major jobs, the education department should prepare 25 presentations justifying the education resources to train each group of employees.

When a curriculum of courses exist for each major job, the education department is able to provide first-line managers and supervisors with simple one- or two-page guidelines on how to plan education for their employees. With a subject-based approach, first-line managers are often given huge education catalogs with hundreds of courses. Neither the managers nor the employees have the time or skill to do curriculum planning. The education department should be responsible for curriculum planning, not the students.

Some companies will tell you they do not do curriculum planning for major jobs because the employees will expect wage increases and promotions when they complete their courses. That is not a valid excuse. Performance on the job, not course completions, is the basis for increases and promotions.

Once again, curriculum planning within major jobs may sound simple and straightforward, but when you try to implement this approach, many people feel you are causing a revolution—which indeed you are, when you consider the way most organizations plan their education.

SUMMARY

When an organization has a course curriculum for each major job, it is easier to make sure that the right person is in the right course at the right time. The number of "professional students" who would sooner be in a classroom than on the job decreases. The number of students attending the wrong classes because of poor planning or selection decreases. Line management's approval of an employee's attending a class takes on a new meaning, because managers now know what classes are essential.

Education managers should make a final check to ensure that the right people are in a course. At the beginning of the class the manager should conduct a survey that asks three questions:

- What is your job?
- Why do you need this training?
- How will you apply the lessons to your job?

Then, everyone—including the students—can be sure that the course will be a sound investment.

7///

The Systems Approach to Education

The previous chapters have discussed breakthrough ideas for raising the quality of education and containing costs. The purpose of this chapter is to help the readers communicate their major strategies to the key audiences that must buy into the recommended changes:

- Executive management
- Line managers and their staffs
- Corporate functional executives and their staffs
- Management teams within education
- Instructors, course developers, and other education department personnel

In almost every organization, hundreds of people make or influence key decisions about education. In a few organizations, the total number is several thousand, including people in operations overseas. Where there is a need for massive change, which is the case in education, people need to see a vision. Where are we going? Why are we doing this? These questions will be asked over and over again.

The majority of people who do not immediately "buy in" to the vision are not people who automatically resist change. They are simply people who do not understand what the leaders of the new programs

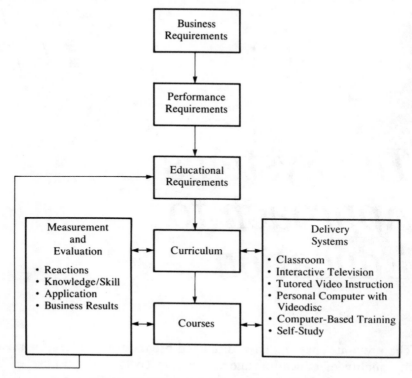

FIGURE 3. A systems approach to education.

have in mind. Massive change involves a massive communications task. The leaders of change must be willing to devote a large part of their time to explaining the value of new education systems.

The initial step in this communications task is to articulate an overall vision to the people who will make it happen. You should be able to present the vision, schematically, on one page. The vision should be discussed in as many meetings as possible and should be included in documents such as guidelines and newsletters. Figure 3 shows the one-page "Systems Approach To Education" chart that represents the vision at IBM. It has been used throughout IBM to articulate how we want to manage education in future years. Why do we call it a *systems approach to education?*

In the 1950s and 1960s, selling computers to large organizations was a major challenge. One method of marketing was called the application approach, which meant selling one application (such as payroll, billing, and accounts receivable) at a time. The other method was called the systems approach, and it involved selling many applications at a time and coordinating them in *information systems.* This meant having an overall picture or vision of how information would flow on computers through an organization, linking all applications and establishing information as a resource. Those who used the systems approach were the sales leaders of the early computer years. The systems approach required executive management involvement and commitment. Some people say the systems approach to education can be traced back to the 1950s, when the military/industrial complex was first trying to bring structure to education. The focus of these activities was to bring order out of the chaos that characterized the design and delivery of instruction at that time.

Today, we are applying the lessons we learned from computers and the experience derived from the application of the systems approach to sell and implement major changes in education. In our environment, we are defining a systems approach to education as a process for developing instruction that is based on defined business requirements and that produces gains in knowledge and skill to improve job performance.

THE SYSTEMS APPROACH AT IBM

Below, I elaborate on each step in the systems approach and also show several practical examples of how this management system works to increase the quality and contain the costs of future education programs.

Business requirements are those specific action programs that must be implemented to achieve goals and strategies. For example, when IBM introduced the original personal computer in 1981, it was essential to properly implement the personal computers within IBM itself. The business requirement for the information systems department can be summarized as follows.

> The function of Information Systems would need to build general purpose, cross-functional applications such as an office system software package for calendar management, word processing, electronic mail, and so on. In addition, they would need to write many specific application programs that would be used in IBM for personal computing.

Performance Requirements are those specific subjects individuals have to know and do in their jobs if the business requirements are to be met. The education department must translate business requirements into performance requirements. This is accomplished by reviewing the major jobs in the company to see what impact the new business requirements have on each job. Another example drawn from IBM—the introduction of the personal computer for use by secretaries—shows the interaction of business and performance requirements. When IBM decided that the personal computer would become the work station for secretaries and that all the other computers and typewriters previously used (e.g., the Displaywriter®, the 5520® computer, electronic typewriters) would be phased out over time, an enormous change was made in the performance requirements of the secretarial job.

Once performance requirements have been determined, planners in the education department must convert them into *education requirements*. This means determining what levels of training are required for specific jobs, based on task and needs analyses. In the example cited above, the education planners might have determined that secretaries needed training in basic computer literacy as well as word processing.

Once the education requirements are documented, the instructional designers convert them into *curriculum design*. For example, if giving personal computers to secretaries involves major new education requirements, new courses will be designed within the curriculum of courses for the secretarial job. If the requirements are minor, the instructional designer might modify some existing courses.

The *course development* work is then performed by a team of experts led by the instructional designers. This is where quality is built into the course.

One of the major decisions in the curriculum and course design is the question of which *delivery system* will achieve the highest quality and most cost-effective course. As you remember from a previous chapter, this decision determines the levels of cost more than does any other decision.

Also, during the curriculum design and course development, *measurements* must be built into the course to be certain the student learns, retains, and is able to apply the lessons of the course.

The alternative to using a systems approach to education is to stay in the world of unstructured education. Many American companies have invested in factory and office automation but are not pleased with the return on their investment. Employees either resist the automation or are just plain confused—all because of a lack of training. Many companies do not fully utilize the power of their personal computers because of deficiencies in their education systems. Many secretaries have not been properly trained on personal computers. Many high-priced professionals in various departments are struggling to use their personal computers effectively. Companies spend millions on hardware and software but fail to invest in the necessary training programs that are the key to successful implementation of the tools in which they have invested so much money.

Some organizations have delivered personal computers to executives' offices. A few executives, who like high-tech tools, have learned how to use them in a productive way, but too often the majority of executives let the computers sit unused in their offices (the world's most expensive paperweights!) until someone takes the initiative to provide a one- or two-day training program. But even these executive training programs are too often crash courses in which the instructor merely tells the executives what keys to hit. Few have recognized the performance requirements of executives vis-à-vis personal computers, much less made the translation to education requirements. Executive training should be one of the major focuses in an organization that needs the benefit of a systems approach to education.

ROLE MODELS

Where is the systems approach to education practiced today? Only a few organizations, such as Arthur Andersen & Co., have implemented this process throughout their organizations. The service organization within IBM provides another role model for using the systems approach.

IBM's customer engineers are responsible for the installation, maintenance, and repair of the company's products. Their training must be outstanding because no one else can fix the machines. The service division offers over 400 courses for customer engineers, who are typically high-school graduates with a two-year associate degree in a related technical area. Each customer engineer is a specialist in a family of machines, which ensures that each engineer has an "embraceable job." Service management does not want to overtrain an engineer on too many machines and thus compromise the high level of skill required for each machine that an engineer is scheduled to work on. New customer engineers receive several weeks of training during the first year on such subjects as installation, maintenance, troubleshooting, upgrading equipment, and writing diagnostic reports. Every year thereafter they receive about 16 days of education, which include eight days in either the Atlanta or the Chicago education center and eight days of computer-based training and self-study courses in a learning center at their branch offices.

Suppose IBM was preparing to announce a new mid-range computer. How would the systems approach to education work in this situation? First, education planners would start translating the new business requirements into performance requirements. For example, they would identify the group of customer engineers that would repair the new mid-size computer. This decision would be made at the plant where the new computer was developed and where it will be manufactured. The performance requirements are then translated into education requirements. When the cost of training several thousand customer engineers on a new computer is estimated, controversy often erupts because the forecasted expense is usually very high. Fortunately for the customer, the preliminary estimate of training costs and the ensuring debate will quite often force development engineers to build more reliability and more sophisticated diagnostic systems into the computer. This will reduce the cost of repairs and also reduce the cost of training customer engineers. It is easy to see from this example how education planning becomes part of the mainstream of a business and should be viewed as a key part of the investment in product development.

When development engineers and education planners have agreed on a set of education requirements, the instructional designers develop outstanding courses at a central location. The courses are delivered over the most cost-effective delivery systems to thousands of customer engineers in the United States and to many more around the globe. This is an example of central planning and course development with decentralized, low-cost delivery systems. (Over the years, IBM has closed a dozen education centers and saved millions of dollars by delivering over 50 percent of its education in branch offices.)

All four levels of measurements are built into the courses. We want to be sure the customer engineer likes the course (level 1), learns the lessons (level 2), applies the lessons (level 3), and contributes to the desired business results (level 4). At IBM, the field managers, who supervise the customer engineers, are held accountable for calls made by untrained personnel, so those situations are extremely rare. The education program is monitored to determine if enhancements introduced later in the product life-cycle will require changes in the curriculum.

The skills planning system and the education system for the service division at IBM have reputations of delivering high quality service while also containing costs. Without these two systems, IBM would employ two or three thousand additional customer engineers at a cost of millions of dollars, because thousands of additional calls and much more time would be required to fix the machines.

Now, I wish I could tell you that every area of the business and every major job at IBM has already achieved benefits similar to those outlined for service training by using the "Systems Approach To Education". Too often in the past, other areas of the business have said that a structured approach is impossible for their "unique" areas. Fortunately, all major areas of IBM are now implementing the systems approach to education and will be achieving the same quality levels and similarly containing their education costs.

The systems approach to education has become the banner for rallying executive support and for communicating the concepts and strategies of the corporate education organization throughout IBM. This includes the central education departments, the 40-plus manufacturing and development sites, and the branch offices overseas. This banner reaches thousands of people involved in education and, in so doing, has communicated the vision of where education at IBM is going.

The systems approach has also provided the framework for linking and integrating successful local programs. For example, the guided-learning centers and the satellite classroom systems that were started in Atlanta and Dallas contribute to the delivery-system box in Figure 3 on page 108. The structured course-development procedures of our finance and planning education center greatly influenced the course development box. The successful curriculum planning work of the information systems education department was the basis for the curriculum box. The tutored video system developed by technical education became another element in the delivery system box. All the outstanding local education procedures and programs were collected through the systems approach to form a grand and new corporatewide education strategy.

Other companies are fine-tuning and modifying the systems approach to education, as they try to bring more structure to their own education programs. The systems approach is not only the vision of where we are going with the new education system; it is the vehicle by which we shall get there. It defines the journey to our goals. Such a journey will usually take five years in most organizations. In very large companies, the journey may take up to ten years. The next step at IBM is to use the systems approach as a model to evaluate progress. Which unit of the business does the best job in curriculum planning? What units need to improve? This will be addressed in Chapter 9, which discusses how to manage education.

SYSTEMS APPROACH AT UNITED WAY

Some people may think that such a structured approach only applies to large, rich organizations like IBM. But a structured approach to education has also helped the United Way of America. In the early 1980s, the chief executive of IBM offered to build a series of training programs for the United Way. The president of the United Way accepted, thinking that he would see some minor enhancements to courses that already existed in the organization's training department.

When education planners at IBM examined the existing United Way courses, it became clear that most of the content was motivational. The courses told volunteers that they should feel good asking for donations to support many worthwhile, not-for-profit organizations. The training included very few lessons on how to do the job of asking for a contribution.

Let's follow the systems approach chart one more time to see how this process works equally well for a not-for-profit organization.

First, the business requirements were easily stated by the United Way management team. The United Way mission is to increase the organized capacity of people to care for one another. The United Way system and its diverse programs are carried out through community fund-raising campaigns at the workplace. The management team wanted to increase the productivity of the paid professional staff and the millions of volunteers responsible for raising the money that supports the thousands of organizations throughout the United States funded by the United Way.

The second step was to convert the United Way's business requirements into performance requirements. To do this, the major jobs in the fund-raising process had to be identified. There were 12:

- Managers of the paid professional staff
- Paid professional staff
- Volunteers

  - Chief executive officers
  - Campaign chairpersons (each company)

- Communications vice chairpersons
- Data and finance vice chairpersons
- Employee solicitation vice chairpersons
- Labor solicitation vice chairpersons
- Training vice chairpersons
- Solicitation captains
- Solicitors
- Loaned executives (*pro bono* hours donated by businesses or professional organizations)

As would be necessary in any organization, a considerable amount of time was spent defining the tasks that each of the 12 jobs had to accomplish if the United Way was to have a successful fund-raising campaign. When the knowledge and skills were identified, the performance requirements were translated into education requirements.

A series of workbooks and videotapes were produced, based on the curriculum design and course development techniques outlined in this book. A cost-effective delivery system was used in which self-paced course materials were provided to local volunteer training departments for implementation.

The results of the training program were far better than those of previous programs because the courses were job-oriented. People who volunteer are no different from people who get paid. They like to know specifically what they must do to be successful. Over 550 local United Way organizations implemented the training program during the first few years. All experienced major increases in giving. Thousands of paid professionals and volunteers were trained. At a luncheon to celebrate the completion of the project, the president of the United Way told the course development team, "I now realize that we have a training program that will not only allow us to be more productive but will also help us to manage the organization more effectively."

SUMMARY

The systems approach to education will work in any organization that has a full-time training department. It works where there is 100 percent classroom training, and it works where there is a mixture of classroom and computer-based training. The systems approach is essential when the executives of an organization decide they want to see a tangible return on their investment in education. No organization ever goes back to unstructured, nonmeasurable education once it has seen the results of using the structured systems approach.

In the past, company training departments have created a bad image for themselves. Historically, they have been viewed as the people with the audiovisual equipment who organize a "rest and recreation" course to give employees a break from the daily pressures of work. They are viewed as being out of the business mainstream. The systems approach changes the image and role of education throughout the entire organization.

I am often asked what three or four management decisions are essential to managing education in the same way that other areas of the business are managed. The answer is easy.

- First, define what education is essential to the health of the organization.

    - Job training courses
    - Development courses for selected employees to enable them to assume positions of greater responsibility

    This is accomplished by identifying the major jobs within the company and then building a curriculum of courses for each job based on task and needs analysis.

- Second, implement measurements to determine if people learn, retain, and apply the lessons.

- Third, raise the quality of the course content and reduce the number of hours per course by implementing instructional design methods for course development.

- Fourth, use cost-effective delivery systems that raise the quality of course content and contain costs at the same time.

A structured approach to education works equally well in centralized organizations and decentralized businesses. Organization structure is important to how a systems approach to education is implemented and is the subject of the next chapter.

8 ///

How to Organize for Accelerated Progress

In most companies, government agencies, and not-for-profit organizations, the action programs described in Chapters 4, 5, and 6 for raising education quality and containing costs cannot be implemented within existing organizational structures.

In many companies, the typical education organization is highly decentralized, with a few instructors reporting to a local education manager. A manufacturing site or a division reporting to functional areas such as personnel, marketing, engineering, information systems, and manufacturing might have as many as three—or six!—education departments. This is the one-room schoolhouse approach to organization, and it never will be cost-effective in today's business environment. In a local, decentralized organization, quality is directly dependent upon each teacher. With hundreds or thousands of teachers "doing their thing" and, no doubt, sincerely believing that they are teaching exactly what the organization needs, the task of setting quality standards, much less maintaining them, is almost impossible.

Other companies have an organization structure that at first seems very logical. A central requirements department tells a central development department what courses should be created for the various education centers. Unfortunately, this model also has problems. The people in the central development department feel they know more about what courses are required than the requirements department. Development redefines the requirements, which means duplicated effort and cost. When the courses are delivered to education centers, the instructors feel they know more about course content than the course developers, leading to still more duplicate effort and cost. It is not unusual to see 50 percent or more of course content redeveloped at the education centers.

The first rule for selecting an organization structure is to design a structure for education that is parallel to the overall corporation, government agency, or not-for-profit organization structure. If the business is very decentralized (for example, if one division makes helicopters and another manufactures china for dining rooms), do not try to build a centralized education organization. On the other hand, many organizations claim to be more decentralized than they actually are. Look at the size of headquarters and you will be able to tell how decentralized the organization is. Some so-called decentralized companies are in fact centralized and really need a new, centralized education function.

In this chapter, I will discuss two common organization patterns for education—decentralized and centralized. Then I will discuss the use of the task-force approach to define an appropriate structure for your organization.

A DECENTRALIZED APPROACH

In this approach, the central education department on the corporate staff could be a separate staff or part of the personnel, or human resources, department. This department should provide a focus on education through activities such as

- Developing a company-wide strategy for education programs
- Developing guidelines for carrying out education programs (for a detailed description of such guidelines, see the next chapter)
- Providing education programs for functions such as personnel (management and employee development) and finance that have common procedures throughout all decentralized divisions
- Sponsoring meetings of division directors of education to encourage sharing new education methods and courses
- Implementing a corporate staff review system to ensure division and corporate management that employee training is in place, is of high quality, and has reasonable costs (division management could use such a review as a "third party opinion")

- Maintaining a relationship with outside professional education organizations to provide guidance for new methods and new delivery systems to the decentralized education departments
- Communicating information about outstanding methods and programs between and among the divisions of the organization
- Setting standards for delivery systems

The corporate staff for education is the glue that holds together the company-wide education activities. A sample approach to a decentralized organization is illustrated in Figure 4. Note that it includes a central education department as a part of the corporate headquarters staff as well as education and training departments in each of the

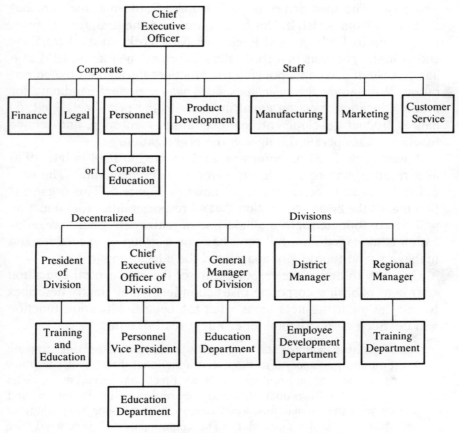

FIGURE 4. A decentralized approach to organizing education.

decentralized divisions or units. As the chart suggests, various titles and department names will be applied throughout a decentralized organization. The education and training department in each division or unit handles all the course requirements for that division or unit. The division president or general manager must hold this department responsible for training all employees in the division.

A CENTRALIZED APPROACH

The second approach to accelerating progress is a centralized education function. IBM–United States provides a good case study. While IBM is known as a decentralized company with many manufacturing, marketing, and service divisions, it really is managed on a centralized basis. The disk drives from San Jose, California, the personal computers from Raleigh, North Carolina, and the mainframes from Poughkeepsie, Endicott, and Rochester, New York, must all work together in the products that IBM sells—information systems. IBM also has consistent personnel policies and practices throughout the corporation. With about 85 basic jobs, IBM was a perfect candidate for a new education function equal in status to the personnel, legal, finance, product development, manufacturing, marketing, and service functions that operate throughout the organization.

A new centralized function was implemented at IBM in late 1986 as a result of an organization task-force recommendation. The centralized education organization is shown in Figure 5. This organization makes the basic assumption that all responsibilities for education will be consolidated into a single line organization. Therefore, education is managed on a full-time basis by a group of executives and managers who thoroughly understand the education business.

One way to define the responsibility of the new central education staff is to publish a corporate instruction letter that clearly describes for all the other business areas what the central education function will do. Such an instruction letter might read like this:

> The corporate functional staff (e.g., manufacturing) will provide strategic direction and guidance to its respective functional director of education to ensure that the curriculum meets its functional requirements. The (manufacturing) functional staff has the responsibility to review and concur with the annual functional education plans, including additions and deletions to the curriculum. The (manufacturing) functional vice president may also have the right to concur in the selection for the director of education, who is named by the vice president of education.

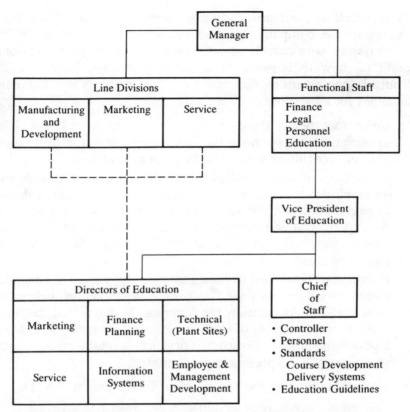

FIGURE 5.   IBM's centralized approach to organizing education.

The functional vice president should also provide assistance to the director of education for recruiting personnel in rotational education assignments.

The instruction letter should also include a section on the responsibility of line management to ensure that the right employees are enrolled in the right courses at the right time. A key item in the instruction letter is a commitment to review the health of education once a year. The review should be made to the management committee or the senior executives.

A small central staff within education is responsible for maintaining control over the assets, finances, and personnel of the education department. In addition, there are two or three small departments that develop guidelines on how to do education, that is, how to develop high quality courses, to implement measurements, and to install cost-effective delivery systems.

The central staff comprises some of the most experienced educators from within the company. They usually will have the responsibility for interfacing with outside organizations in order to gain additional insight on how to improve the education process. Here is a list of outside organizations that could be your partners in developing guidelines for education:

- *Universities.* Select three or four outstanding schools that have strong graduate programs for instructional design plus a record of doing consulting work with large organizations.
- *Consultants.* If your organization is spending millions of dollars on employee training, an investment of a few thousand dollars to gain an independent viewpoint will be well worth the money. An experienced and unbiased consultant could tell your organization where your program strengths are and what areas need improvement.
- *Professional Education Organizations.* At this time, the education community does not have one overall organization such as the American Bar Association, the American Medical Association, or the American Institute of Certified Public Accountants. A strong, highly influential, and respected organization may emerge out of several very good present organizations:

  - American Society for Training and Development (ASTD)
  - National Society for Performance and Instruction (NSPI)
  - Society for Applied Learning Techniques (SALT)
  - Association for Education Communications and Technology (AECT)
  - Association for Development of Computer-based Instructional Systems (ADCIS)

- *Education Course Development Companies.* As discussed in Chapter 2, this group of companies, which is often represented by the Instructional Systems Association, employs some of the most qualified educators. They constitute a very valuable information source, bringing years of experience to bear on a diversity of issues and problems.

Apart from the small central staff, the vast majority of the education personnel in IBM's centralized organization are in the six large functional education departments:

- Marketing
- Service (maintenance of equipment)
- Finance and planning
- Information and office systems
- Technical (engineering, programming, manufacturing)
- Employee and management development

Within these functional areas, each director of education is responsible for 3 to 30 of the major jobs in the IBM Corporation. The responsibilities of a functional director of education are to

- Develop a course curriculum for each major job
- Conduct needs and cost analysis for new courses
- Work with the corporate functional vice president and staff to obtain agreement on a curriculum of courses by job
- Work with line management to achieve similar agreement
- Develop the courses in the most cost-effective manner, whether central classroom, satellite classroom, local site classroom, learning center (computer-based training), or work station (systems delivered education)
- Eliminate duplicate courses and ensure that there are no voids in education

At first, directors of education in the functional areas may not see the new organization as embodying a major change. Once they see their new list of responsibilities, however, they will realize that there has been a revolution in education.

As you can see, this centralized organization avoids split responsibility, which often means no responsibility. The new functional approach to organizing education sends a strong message to everyone that employee education is important. Now there is a line organization to get the job done. The focus is on education to perform. The grand strategy is in place, and the debate is over. The details of specific action programs and implementation success stories are all that the executives want to hear after this type of organization decision is made. Education is no longer a sideshow; it is in the mainstream of the organization.

This centralized approach to education organization will also work well within a division of a large corporation or government agency.

If a company selects a centralized line organization for education, all of education and training should be brought under the auspices of a vice president of education. The vice president and his or her management team should be given the resources and complete responsibility for training all employees to do their jobs and for developing selected employees for jobs or greater responsibility. This team must have the ability to do tradeoff planning. For example, finding a more cost-effective way to carry out manufacturing education should mean that more money can, if necessary, be spent on marketing education. Or the money saved after an initial investment in cost-effective delivery systems could be used to fund new courses and new delivery systems. If parts of the education organization stay within other line organization areas, the central education department will have a major problem in gathering the funds to invest in new courses, because the money saved at local education centers will never be directly available to invest in new courses and new delivery systems elsewhere. Tradeoff planning is the answer for funding change within education. If all of education is in one line organization, tradeoff resource planning is feasible.

An important decision to be made concerns whom the vice president of education should report to. Everyone with significant responsibility wants to report to the chief executive officer, but often in larger organizations this many direct-reports is not practical or possible. In many organizations, the CEO has a senior or executive vice president in charge of the legal, public relations, government relations, and personnel departments. This senior vice president is an appropriate person for the vice president of education to report to. In other companies, there is an executive vice president of human resource development (HRD), and the head of education may report to him or her. This is also appropriate if the HRD function is considered a part of the line organization. Too often, however, HRD is a corporate staff function that handles only compensation plans, equal opportunity programs, benefit plans, and industrial relations. If that is the case, education can become too far removed from the executive team that runs the business on a day-to-day basis. When the operating line executives learn the value of a trained employee, versus the problems and inaccuracies created by an untrained employees, they want the education vice president at their meetings.

No matter what organizational decisions are made, the final key to success is the quality of the person selected to lead education. This person must be a leader who can create a vision toward which the education organization works. The management of change requires a vice president of education who has the confidence and professional respect of the other executive team members; they must believe that the leader of education knows the business and can work with them.

The vice president of education needs basic general management skills; these are actually more important than specific education expertise. Of course, the senior executive of education must become knowledgeable about education. Fortunately, there are plenty of people who can educate him or her on education issues. Because it takes time to fully grasp all the issues, the leader of education must be willing to commit at least five years to the job. Managing change is extremely difficult if the leadership is changing every two years.

THE ORGANIZATION STUDY

How do you sell an organization study for education? In most companies, you will not have to sell the study if your executive presentation shows the education cost and presents a proposed management system like the systems approach discussed in the previous chapter. When the executives see how much is being spent on education and they make the decision to manage this part of their company like other areas of the business, they will ask for an organization study. If they do not request the study, the director of education should ask for approval to perform one. The study requires a task force to determine how education should be organized to accelerate progress from unstructured education to structured education. The following pages will describe the objectives for an organization study, the membership of the task force, and an agenda for the task force that is built around six meetings.

Objectives for an organization study

Objectives of the new organization should be clear as you request the study and embark on the task force effort. Here are five sample objectives:

1. Ensure adequate training and education.
   - Provide a curriculum of courses for each major job in the business.
   - Provide development courses for employees who have the potential to be given jobs of greater responsibility.

2. Maximize quality within education.

- Implement instructional-designed courses with appropriate exercises, tests, and measurements.
- Implement an annual review on the health of the education program.
- Develop personnel within education.

3. Implement cost containment programs.

- Implement cost-effective delivery systems.
- Control sourcing of outside resources, such as course materials and instructors.
- Implement central course development.
- Fully utilize existing facilities.

4. Increase management control.

- Include education in the annual operating plan, which involves the budget cycle.
- Establish a common enrollment/administration system.
- Achieve consistent and complete education statistics.

5. Develop a working partnership between education and the corporate functional staffs as well as line management.

Membership of the task force

The task force should be commissioned by the chief executive officer, a senior vice president, or the vice president in charge of the company-wide organizational structure. The task force chairperson should either be the current director of education or a person who could become the director of education. The chairperson should feel that he or she will have the responsibility and ability to implement the task force recommendations.

As in every other important study, the chairperson must be a leader who has the respect of all task-force members. The leader must be sure all views are heard and that decisions are made in such a way that everyone feels he or she has had a fair say. The leader should not disclose a bias, which is difficult to do because the leader usually has deep convictions. He or she should be certain that meetings begin promptly and insist that the members do not try to do their other work while the task force is meeting.

An assistant or deputy chairperson should be named who will be responsible for organizing the meetings, preparing agenda, handling logistics, and taking minutes. This person summarizes the task-force work at the end of the meeting or at the beginning of the next meeting. The chairperson's leadership role is so demanding that an assistant chairperson is essential for assembling the work of the task force into meaningful conclusions and recommendations. The deputy chairperson should also be a leader, but should be somewhat less visible than the chairperson at the meetings. The deputy chairperson will be less actively involved in the major discussions because he or she serves as the listener who will help shape the decisions based on the group's discussions and will develop reports for the final meeting summaries. Basically, this person is the general manager for the work efforts and the final documented reports.

A small task force of four or five persons has the advantage of facilitating decision-making and progress. However, training is found in every major area of the organization. Therefore, a small task force is impractical if you want the major business areas to support the recommended organization for education and training. A typical task force will have ten to twenty members and should include these people:

- Directors or managers of the major education departments
- Executives of each major functional staff area
- Executives of each major line organization

You achieve a higher involvement level if the assignment represents only 50 percent of each member's time. The task force should be completed in 90 days. Allow 30 days to schedule the events and clear calendars for the meetings and work assignments. Allow 60 days for six two-day meetings with work assignments between the meetings.

Task-force meetings

A sample structure for the series of task-force meetings follows.

Each of the six meetings must have a clear set of purposes. Here are the purposes of the first meeting:

- Introduction of task force members
- Kick-off message from a senior executive
- Agreement on organization study objectives
- Agreement on issues to be studied
- Agreement on schedule and meeting dates
- Review of the current organization and mission

The following list presents typical issues a task force will study. Presentations should be due at the second, third, and fourth meetings.

- The relation of skills planning to education planning
- Needs analysis and the requirements process
- Student audiences by major jobs
- Retraining requirements
- Course development procedures/practices
- Current and planned use of cost-effective delivery systems
- Charge-out systems (tuition, etc.)
- Current interface with corporate functional staffs
- Current interface with line management
- Current operating plan budgets
- Student housing
- Administration within education centers
- Enrollment procedures and systems
- Use of university courses
- Interface with universities
- Interface with education development companies
- Contract and purchasing procedures
- Education research and technology

Task-force members should be divided into teams of two or three persons to work on the issues. Each team should take four to six issues and report on one or two issues per meeting. This approach forces involvement by all task-force members and is a great exercise in team building. In addition, this method will bring all members of the task force up to a common knowledge base and will allow new or more creative members to influence the final decisions.

One rule that must be made clear at the first meeting is that organization charts will not be drawn up before the fifth meeting. This is a difficult rule to follow because many task-force members will come to the meeting thinking they could draw the final organization chart within 24 hours. You do not want to make organizational decisions until all task-force members fully understand the issues. You want new thinking on the critical education issues. You must avoid having the "old guard of education" selling the old solutions for the future, which would mean business as usual. Everyone must leave their old baggage outside the door. The task force must have a foundation of facts to support the organizational recommendations that will be made to executive management.

Meetings 2, 3, and 4 are important for the discussion of the issues. Here are the purposes for each of those meetings:

- Second meeting:
  - Presentations on one-third of the issues (start, if possible, with the issues where there is more agreement).
  - Review the status of all work assignments.
  - Add any additional issues to be studied.

- Third meeting:
  - Presentations on one-third of the issues (these may have required work during the past 30 days to develop good presentations).
  - Review the status of work assignments for the next meeting.
  - Add any additional issues to be studied.

- Fourth meeting:
  - Presentations on the final third of the issues (these should be the most challenging decisions, but by the fourth meeting the group should be working well together because they have a much greater understanding of the major issues facing the education management).
  - Outline key organization decisions required for the next meeting.

Each topic should come to closure before the meeting is over. You should try to avoid "carry overs" or "come backs" if the task force is to complete its work on time. Every presentation and work effort should be documented, organized, and provided to the task-force members.

The big meeting is the fifth meeting. During the morning, the group should be divided into three teams (let's call them 1, 2, and 3). Each team is given the same list of five to ten organization decisions to be resolved. For example, one decision might involve where the course development department should report. The list of organization decisions is required because you want each of the three teams to present a solution for each of the decisions.

After the three teams have discussed the organization decisions and made recommendations, which usually takes about three hours, each team must present its recommendations to the entire task force. The task-force members may ask questions to help themselves to understand a recommendation, but no other discussion of the recommendation should be permitted until all three teams have presented. This allows the chairperson to see how much agreement there is between the three teams. It is to be hoped that 40 to 60 percent of the decisions can be agreed on in the first round of decision-making.

The chairperson uses two easel charts or chalkboards to summarize the agreed-upon decisions and the decisions that require more discussion. The task-force members are usually surprised to find out how much agreement there is, but this is the logical result of running a structured task force over several weeks.

After lunch, the teams are restructured. Teams A, B, and C each have members of teams 1, 2, and 3 from the first round. This mixing ensures that each first-round viewpoint is represented in each of the new teams. The new teams are given two hours in which to work on the remaining issues. Though these usually amount to fewer than half the issues of the morning round, these decisions are more difficult to make.

By midafternoon, the three teams should be ready to present their recommendations. Hopefully, half of the decisions in round 2 are now agreed upon. By the first day's end, 70 to 85 percent of the organization decisions are made, and the task force members can feel positive about the work accomplished that day.

In the morning of the second day, the chairperson can lead a discussion of the last two or three decisions to be made or have a third round for the team members. In most situations, the organization decisions have been made by noon of the second day. This permits the task force to begin an outline for the executive presentation that will recommend the new organization.

The sixth meeting is held to communicate the decisions that have been made. The various sections of the executive presentation are assigned to members of the task force at the end of the fifth meeting. Task-force participants arrive at the sixth meeting with real enthusiasm because now all the work comes together for a presentation to the senior executives. The presentation must include

- The objectives of the organization study
- The key issues to be resolved by the recommended organization, such as

  - Improved curriculum planning by major jobs within the organization

- Improved development to raise the quality of course content through the use of instructional design techniques
- Implementation of measurements to ensure the students learn, retain, and apply the lessons
- Greater use of cost-effective delivery systems, including personal tutoring systems in the learning centers
- The implementation schedule (several phases)
- Concerns and risks involved with the new organization
- Overall benefits of the new organization

The executive presentation should be given on the final day of the sixth meeting to the executive who commissioned the task force. At this presentation, a list of other executive reviews should be agreed upon.

The final agenda item is to thank all the task-force members for their hard work, creativity, and dedication to a challenging assignment.

SUMMARY

At a board of governors meeting at ASTD headquarters, an informal discussion was held on how to elevate education to a full functional line organization, such as this chapter has just described. Participants agreed that it usually happens because of one of these factors:

1. The chief executive officer finally realizes the value of training employees and calls for a strong new education organization.
2. External pressures, such as international competition, force a crisis. For example, executives realize that a competitive organization has a highly trained workforce that produces higher quality products or services at lower cost.
3. The education management team has the knowledge required to sell executive management on the need for a more effective education organization to train employees.

This discussion among education executives who represented many large, successful companies concluded that the CEO's decision was the factor that elevated education to an important organization level in the vast majority of cases. There were a few examples of foreign or domestic competition having forced the issue. IBM was one of the companies cited in which the education management team led the effort for a strong new education organization.

In the future, in most organizations there will be a requirement to accelerate progress to a more structured education system that utilizes cost effective delivery systems. This fundamental change requires a critical mass of resources. At that time, many directors of education will need to communicate to their executive teams the importance of a strong educational organization. The lessons outlined in this chapter should help the education leaders to do just that.

9 ///

Measurements and the Management of Education

When the IBM management team learned that IBM's education expenses were about $900 million, they made an immediate demand for accountability. What was the intended return on this multimillion-dollar investment? How good was all this education? What would happen if 25 percent were eliminated? The penetrating questions came fast. It was an uncomfortable feeling to have only measurements of quantity, such as student days and student completions, to present to executives. It quickly became clear that measurements are the essential element of managing education. If executives are to view education as an investment rather than an expense, it must be managed like any other part of the business. Once the decision is made to treat education as an investment, a major effort to install a comprehensive management system, with measurable results, must follow.

GUIDELINES FOR MANAGING EDUCATION

The first step toward managing education is to establish guidelines on how various aspects of the education process should be implemented. Differing opinions on how to approach the major parts of the education process are readily available from books, professional journals, speeches, seminars, and consultants.

During the years that education at IBM was decentralized, there was an opportunity to try every idea and education theory, and that is exactly what happened. Therefore, IBM needed guidelines for education as much as any organization. Six reasons were identified for investing in a two-year effort to develop a series of carefully documented guidelines:

1. With multiple locations, IBM needed common definitions in order to achieve effective communication among all education departments.

2. If IBM was to make a successful transition from an unstructured to a structured approach to education, it needed guidelines to define and help shape a systems approach to education.

3. The managers and employees working in education needed "how to" information from the guidelines to enhance their programs.

4. Before a comprehensive set of measurements could be implemented, IBM needed procedures and methods that were agreed upon and consistent.

5. IBM's thousands of managers, instructors, developers, and support personnel needed guidelines for reference on a day-to-day basis, particularly during the early years of centralized education.

6. The company needed to avoid the waste in cost and time that occurs when one department cannot benefit from the experience of another because of lack of knowledge. For example, why have every department do "pioneering" work in self-study when two departments have had over ten years of successful experience, with several hundred courses to show for their efforts.

Writing the guidelines

The directors of education representing the 15 largest education organizations at IBM identified the major subjects to be covered by the guidelines. Then the directors were asked to send their most knowledgeable person on each subject to a meeting on that subject. For example, we asked each director, "Who in your organization knows the most about measuring education?" The person selected to attend the meeting on measurement and evaluation guidelines discussed the current measurement practices and procedures in his or her area of education. Two or three experts from outside IBM were also asked to give their best thinking on the topic. Next, a member of the corporate education staff worked with the key subject matter experts identified during the meeting to draft the guidelines. A second meeting was held to review the draft, and as much as 30 percent of the guidelines were revised as a result of the second meeting.

Building the guidelines was a major effort, but the approach resulted in the feeling that everyone had been given a voice in the development. The degree to which the guidelines have been used has surprised most people. Rather than gathering dust, they are consulted on a day-to-day basis in all the major departments of education at IBM.

The guidelines developed at IBM

A set of nine guidelines was developed to aid in the implementation and management of a structured education system. Here is a brief description of each.

- *Curriculum planning and development.* This guideline provides an analytical approach to defining the business need for a new curriculum and is required to implement the action programs described in Chapter 6. You might recall that a curriculum plan is the vehicle for training employees within each major job category.
- *Education delivery systems.* This guideline helps managers, developers, and instructors understand and select the most appropriate delivery systems for instructional programs. It is the basis for achieving the cost containment programs outlined in Chapter 4.
- *Course development.* Regardless of which delivery system is selected, the management system to guide course development is basically the same. The six-step course development process was discussed in Chapter 5. The steps are

  - Analysis (task analysis for major job)
  - Course design
  - Development (writing, programming, etc.)
  - Audiovisual, computer program, and print production
  - Implementation
  - Evaluation

This process is essential to raising the quality of education.

- *Measurement and evaluation.* This guideline provides the "how to" processes for implementing the measurement of quality. The four levels of measurement, listed here, are reviewed in this chapter.

  - Reactions
  - Knowledge/skill
  - Application
  - Business results

- *Administrative planning and support for education.* In a typical education center, about 25 percent of education personnel are involved in administration and information-systems jobs. The difference between an outstanding education center and a so-so education center is often the quality of support provided for its operation, and this guideline describes all the key tasks within the support jobs.

- *Instructor training and development.* As a result of applying the systems approach to education, IBM determined that three of the major jobs in education (education manager, instructor, and course developer) themselves required a curriculum of courses to ensure that quality standards were being established and implemented. This guideline outlined the structure of the courses to be developed.

- *Planning education facilities.* IBM has recently built several education centers. This guideline captures the knowledge and experience gained to assure the design of outstanding education facilities in the future. It has also been useful in guiding the remodeling of many existing education centers.

- *Transition programs.* This guideline has been essential to IBM in the 1980s because of the large number of retraining programs. IBM is a full-employment company and does not lay off employees because of new products, new strategies, or new organizations. When there is a surplus of people in one operating unit, IBM moves work to those people or asks the employees to move to other IBM locations that require additional workers. In either case, a need for some retraining programs usually exists. A successful transition program requires a partnership between line management, personnel, education, and communications. This guideline describes each partner's responsibilities so that each program is a success and can be based on past successful transition programs. Transition training is simplified, of course, when a curriculum exists for every major job in the organization.

- *Management of education resources.* This guideline was written to consolidate information that is important for a successful education management system. The topics discussed will be highlighted later in this chapter.

MANAGING AND MEASURING EDUCATION

After all the guidelines were published, a number of other projects were essential to bring education under a single management system.

- *Implement a companywide education strategy.* Education goals must support the overall organization goals. Once education goals have been established, there usually are three to five strategies to reach each goal. Each major education area should document its annual action programs to support these strategies. Having an overall strategy represents another giant step forward to blending all the education departments into a common management and measurement system. Strategy documents are later used for the overall measurement of the health of the education system.
- *Develop an annual budget/operating plan.* Education must participate in the organization's operating plan process. Every area that requires education should submit its plan to the head of education for approval. This will ensure that the entire management team will focus on education and possess meaningful measurements of the total costs involved.
- *Implement facility utilization reports.* Education centers are extremely expensive. In many ways, managing a center is like managing an airline. Every seat that is empty causes the per-student cost of education to rise. Educators like to operate at a comfortable utilization level, and too many seats go unused unless there is a reporting system in place. The measurement of utilization lowers the cost of education.
- *Implement monthly financial and operating measurements.* These reporting systems will vary within each organization, but the typical measurements are headcount, operating budget, student completions, and student days. Yes, there are quantity measures which are equally as important as quality measurements. They tell what quantity of work will be provided based on budgets.

- *Implement a common enrollment/administrative system.* All the courses offered in an organization should be listed in a common database with a common course-numbering system. With such a system, enrollment can be completed from local field offices and manufacturing sites through the corporate network or communication system by keying only once the employee number, the course number, and class date. All other information should be available from the common personnel and education databases. The system will provide class rosters, name tags, name signs, case study lists, instructor schedules, and measurement reports.

- *Establish delivery system strategies/implementation plans.* All major delivery systems require an overall strategy supported by justifications that make good business sense. Once approved, implementation plans usually run from one to three years. The objective is to set standards and implement common delivery systems that enable each course to be developed only once (utilizing the most cost-effective system) rather than multiple times for multiple delivery systems. The volume of student days required by each delivery system is a key measurement for lowering the cost of education.

- *Define career paths, job descriptions, and position evaluations.* If you want to achieve a significant increase in employee morale within the education departments, this is an area on which to spend time and effort. Typically, it involves extending existing job descriptions throughout the education organization on a consistent basis and implementing a structure that creates career paths.

- *Implement a company-wide placement program for education employees.* When important positions open, the most competitive candidates from all education areas should be considered. This is another program that raises morale among educators; it requires a measurement system for personnel placement.

- *Establish communications between all education departments.* A newsletter or professional journal should be established to communicate success stories, key personnel appointments, reorganizations, and information on professional subjects, such as the results of new delivery systems. An annual meeting of all educators within an organization may be a worthwhile investment.

- *Establish an education technology council.* New ideas, teaching methods, and delivery systems are always coming up. These need to be studied and evaluated. When too many people do this work, "reinvention" is too often the result. An education technology council will focus on new programs and help ensure measurable results from new pilot programs.

- *Conduct meetings with external education groups.* There is much to learn from other education groups. The time required to meet with external groups should be carefully controlled to ensure that the right people are in the meetings and that important subjects are on the agenda. This is also true of the time invested in meeting with representatives of professional organizations such as ASTD, NSPI, and SALT. Measuring your own operations against the recommendations of other leaders of employee education is essential to learning how to improve while avoiding the cost of having to invest every new idea yourselves.

- *Implement instructional system design.* Standards must be established and a quality control system implemented to be certain that students learn, retain, and apply the lessons from their training. To do this, an in-depth audit must be made of each course curriculum. All courses should have *level 1* measurements—that is, the reaction of students to course content and logistics should be measured. This tells you whether the students like the course and how much they think the course addresses the objectives to be taught. Level 1 measurements also give you valuable feedback on the overall operations of the education center. The vast majority of courses should also have level 2 measurements, which evaluate whether students have learned the knowledge and skills a course has been designed to teach. Use a pretest to determine whether the course is necessary and to measure the knowledge level of the students before they attend the course. Use a post-test at the end of the course to determine if the students have learned the lessons. Such tests do not need to be validated to the same level as tests used to evaluate employee performance. The intent is to test learning, not to rank students. Note that IBM has found that there is very little correlation between scores on level 1 feedback sheets and level 2 post-tests. You might think that if a student likes a course, he or she will test well, but this is not necessarily the case.

If curricula are planned by major jobs, as described in Chapter 6, most lessons can be subsequently evaluated to determine whether students apply the learning to the job. If curricula are planned by general subject area, it is much more difficult to measure application. Some courses can be measured against business results, but only do this type of measurement if you have solid numbers. Do not use weak data or make assumptions to fake a measurement because this will destroy the credibility of your management system. Too many "return on investment" measurements have been built on a quicksand of assumptions.

A WORD OF CAUTION

Some people get carried away with measurements. Lowering the cost per student day can be a dangerous measurement because it can easily lead to a disregard for quality. If you only want to lower the cost per student day, fill an auditorium with 400 students for five days and run cheap videotapes.

Some years ago, when I was responsible for the sales school in IBM, I noticed that the number of students graduating from sales school was lower than the number of employees being assigned to new sales territories. At the time, a quarterly report went out to the 250 IBM branch managers telling them how their trainees ranked at sales school. A copy of the report, which ranked branch offices by the performance of their students, was sent to the 14 district managers. After investigating the situation, I found out that district managers were putting pressure on the trainees to be the top performers at sales school. The pressure became so great that students quit listening to the oustanding lectures in the morning and just sat and worried about their evaluated sales calls, which were scheduled for the afternoon and which were the basis for evaluating their overall performance at sales school. Worse yet, some trainees with lower qualifications were being held out of sales school because of the report on ranking, meaning that the trainees who most needed the training went directly into their territories without the benefit of sales school.

The problem was fixed by a new system in which grades were limited to "pass with honors," "pass," and "fail" and in which the ranking of branch managers by trainee performance was eliminated. This was a classic case of too many measurements.

SUMMARY

Despite the story just related, the problem normally is that there are too few measurements in education. This is beginning to change because the organizations that have the most measurements have the most resources for education. Executives will support additional personnel and funds if they know that course results are going to be measured.

The salaries paid to education directors and managers are usually influenced by the level and results of measurements. Salaries have grown dramatically for education executives where the measurements that answer the following questions are in place:

1. Are the key jobs within the organization identified?
2. Do curricula exist for every major job?
3. Are education curriculum guidelines for each major job available to line managers?
4. Are inventories available for trained and untrained employees?
5. Were the courses developed with instructional design techniques to ensure high quality and, where possible, to reduce course length in order to reduce time away from the job?
6. Have cost-effective delivery systems been implemented?
7. Are students measured on whether they learn, retain, and apply the lessons?
8. Are the education facilities fully utilized?
9. Is education within the allocated budget?
10. Is there adequate administrative support?
11. Are staff development programs in place?
12. Do executives and line managers have confidence in the education program?

In some organizations, the executive in charge of education has implemented a formal annual education review with the executive management team. An annual executive meeting focusing on education is the final step in achieving a true partnership between education and executive management. This review system helps to ensure a balance between measurements of the quality and the quantity of education. At IBM, we refer to this annual presentation, which is designed to answer the questions listed above, as the "Health of Education."

10 ///

Five Phases for Managing Change in Education

Too often, education reformers want to start at ground zero and invent an entire new education system. A more practical approach is to start with outstanding aspects of existing education programs and let them serve as the role models.

In many organizations today you will find examples of outstanding education and training programs that are all too often isolated and unnoticed. At IBM in the early 1980s, the following leading-edge programs were in place or being planned throughout the company:

- *The service organization* had invested many years in computer-based training. Its courses were on a central computer, and the students (customer engineers) could receive up-to-date course content over the network. The central computer maintained records showing which courses the students had completed. No other IBM area had a similar system because such an advanced system was viewed as a special requirement for service education. Today, everyone realizes that such systems are necessary for all major areas of the company.

- *The marketing education group* had developed a guided learning center where highly structured self-study courses were administered. All other areas of IBM agreed that the learning center filled a unique marketing requirement, but they also claimed that such facilities were not appropriate for their own parts of the company. Today, IBM is trying to install structured education learning centers throughout its organization.

- *The service and information systems education group* had designed curricula based on jobs. We now know that this approach is essential for all major education departments.
- *Marketing* had developed a satellite classroom system. *Technical education* was inventing another satellite system, and the *information systems* and *finance and planning* departments were creating still another system. IBM now has two satellite systems, with plans to consolidate their activities into one system.

It was obvious to some of us at IBM that all the "islands" of outstanding programs and projects had to be brought together under a company-wide management system for education. Once again, this might sound like a simple thing to do, but, as you have read, a company-wide education system is a very challenging goal to achieve.

THE NEED FOR A TRANSFORMATIONAL LEADER

It is important to build on the successful programs that already exist in an organization, but do not underestimate the resistance that you will face as you try to transfer successful programs elsewhere throughout the organization. As you start down the road toward achieving an education system that serves the entire organization, you must be able to sell major change. Some people will call it massive change.

In their 1986 book, *The Transformational Leader*, authors Noel M. Tichy (a University of Michigan professor and former director of General Electric's Management Development Institute) and Mary Anne Devanna (a professor at Columbia University) used the framework of a three-act play to explain the transformational issues organizations face and the actions required to bring about change. They called Act 1 "Recognizing the Need for Revitalization." Because many organizations are witnessing more progress today within employee education and training programs than at any time in the past, it is easy to miss the need for revitalization. Unfortunately, most organizations will take 25 years to accomplish what they must do during the next five years to develop and maintain a competitive workforce. I hope this book will help many organizations recognize the need for revitalization.

Tichy and Devanna call Act 2 "Creating a Vision." Chapter 7 of this book, on the systems approach to education, shows how the vision that has been successful at IBM for the past five years was created.

Tichy and Devanna call Act 3 "Institutionalizing Change." Chapters 3 through 9 of this book are aimed at showing how to institutionalize change within the organization's employee training function.

A transformational issue faced by many organizations in the 1950s and 1960s was how to effectively install information systems, that is, how to restructure a company for the world of data processing. Looking back on those early days in the information systems industry, it is clear that every organization that made progress with computers had to find a transformation leader who could convince people of the need for revitalization or change. The same person had to create a vision to implement what was to become the massive change brought by new on-line terminal database information systems. In many cases, that person eventually became the information systems vice president.

Normally, an organization has very few transformational leaders. Most managers are good at supervising existing procedures and operations. Organizations must look for managers who can create, sell, and implement change. An organization must include leadership qualities (which too often are not emphasized enough) in its succession planning process. Those outstanding managers who have the added ability to become transformational leaders should be candidates for future executive positions in the organization.

Every organization that employs more than 5,000 people should be looking for a transformational leader to head the employee education and training function. It will be a very challenging job because there will be great pressure to achieve results in the 1990s. Most managers will fail. Only a leader will succeed.

PEOPLE WILL RESIST CHANGE

As they do in other areas, many people will resist change in education. Let me describe some of these people.

First, there is the "positive" resister. This person agrees with all the new ideas and programs, but never takes the first step to implement any changes.

Then there is the "unique" resister. All this change is good for the other education areas, but it clearly doesn't apply to that individual's unique education department.

We all know the "let me be last" resister. This person will not say your ideas are wrong. His or her strategy is to be the last department to implement changes, hoping that all these new ideas will die out before his or her department must move forward into the new world.

The "we need more time to study" resister is very common. This is one of the most palatable reasons for resisting. After all, who could object to doing more studies?

The "states rights" resister is also common in large companies. This person always resists any programs from headquarters, making great presentations about how local programs are the only effective way to go.

The "cost justifier" wants everything cost-justified prior to any change. This resister demands to have "business cases" prepared. The real messsage this person sends, however, is a simple resistance to change.

One of the most difficult people to win over to a new system is the "incremental change" resister. This is the person who will try anything new as long as the new system has everything the old system had.

The vast majority of resisters eventually buy into the systems approach to education. One test of your vision is to watch the last of the resisters leave for jobs outside education. If they do not become believers, they usually leave because more and more people around them start to believe in the vision. The challenge is not to look too pleased as the final holdouts depart the scene. The resisters do serve a purpose. The resisters force the visionary to constantly sharpen the vision. They force many system improvements.

EMPOWERING THE EDUCATORS

Empowerment is a term that is frequently used in the discussion of restructuring education. Too many people underestimate the desire of educators to contribute to major improvements in the process of learning. Once the instructors see the power of instructional design and measurements to bring about more learning, greater respect for instructors, and more resources to do the job, they become a great positive force for change. Teachers and course developers want to be part of an outstanding education organization. Morale goes up at almost the same rate as the increase in the quality of courses.

Instructors at IBM today can see the value of alternative delivery systems. They are comfortable working with a combination of self-study, personal tutoring, and classroom teaching. They see that

IBM's executives have a much higher level of respect for the overall education function within the company. With new career paths and the proper compensation plans, no educator feels like a second-class citizen within employee education. Educators know they comprise an essential part of what makes the company operate and grow.

MEASURING PROGRESS

The transformational leader's demand for progress must be balanced with patience. If you try to move too fast, you can create a real backlash against the new strategies and programs. Smaller organizations should be able to implement a systems approach to education in five years. Large organizations will require eight to ten years. No one should be discouraged by the length of time. It took IBM two years to move clearly from Act 1 (recognize the need for revitalization) into Act 2 (create a new vision). Act 2 required about one year to implement. Act 3 (institutionalizing change) will require an estimated five years.

Measurable results can be obtained during every year of the process. More importantly, the major breakthroughs can be obtained within a couple of years.

To make progress, a measurement system must be instituted to show the transformation within each area of education. Who are the leaders moving toward a systems approach? Who is in the middle, and who is barely moving yet?

Management levers to obtain progress

After reading education journals, attending many seminars, and listening to "the experts," I have concluded that management can use six major levers of action against which progress can be measured. They are

1. *Ensure a business need.* Remember Chapters 3 and 4, which showed how an education department must work with corporate functional staffs and line management to establish the true business requirements for employee education and training. Implement a needs and cost analysis for each course.
2. *Ensure that the right person is in the right course.* This concept was explained in Chapter 6. The major jobs must be identified, and a course curriculum designed for each major job. Guidelines showing these curricula must be documented for managers and

employees. These guidelines permit an annual employee development plan that includes education. Finally, there must be a database for recording and reporting the training level for every employee.

3. *Implement quality measurements.* In Chapter 5, the key lesson was implementing levels of measurement to ensure that the students learn, retain, and apply the course lessons. Remember, every ten minutes of a course must be outstanding. Courses should be modified and improved until the vast majority of students pass with high achievement scores.

4. *Develop new courses only once.* This lesson, from Chapter 5, is especially important for large organizations, which run a great risk of wasting time and money on duplicate or multiple development efforts at various locations. Oustanding courses also eliminate the need to reteach a subject to the same person at a later time.

5. *Implement ISD (Instructional Systems Design) within course development.* The advantages of using instructional design methods to reduce the length of the course and to increase the quality of the course were described in Chapter 5.

6. *Implement cost-effective delivery systems.* Chapter 4 discussed this subject. Remember, this is the area where an organization can see the greatest impact on quality and cost containment. A large amount of education can be delivered via self-study, computer-based training, and interactive videodiscs, eliminating travel and living costs while reducing the number of education centers, instructors, and support personnel.

A five-phase system to measure progress

A five-phase system can be instituted to measure progress on these six levers.

Phase 1: Unstructured education. This environment characterized employee education in almost every organization prior to the 1980s. Here is a summary of unstructured education, as described in an earlier chapter:

- Hundreds of courses exist to cover major subject areas (thousands in large companies).
- Job-oriented curricula do not exist.
- Needs and cost analyses do not exist.

- A majority of course development is performed by instructors during off-hours when they are not teaching; there is no instructional design.
- Measurements are primarily of quantity and rarely of quality.
- The vast majority of courses are classroom lectures.
- Management is not involved with education.

Phase 2: Inventory of education programs and costs. Management requests an inventory of education programs and a complete cost study for all education, training, and development courses. In this phase, management might even ask a consulting firm to review the organization's education programs comparing current practices against a list of best practices within the employee education industry.

Phase 3: Planning, measurement and organization. Management must determine how to implement a structured, systems approach to education. An internal task force or an education consultant could do an organization study for this purpose. This would permit the six levers of education management to be installed to achieve these three objectives:

1. Offer only essential courses to meet business requirements
2. Ensure the courses are the highest quality
3. Implement programs to contain education costs

This phase includes the development of an education measurement system that balances both quality and quantity. The final work in phase 3 is to establish goals for employee education, a strategic plan to meet those goals, and action programs to get started.

Phase 4: Implementing structured education. Each major area of the organization is now on the road to establishing the following conditions:

- Training is defined by business requirements.
- Major jobs are defined.
- A course curriculum exists for each major job.
- Needs and cost analyses exist for each new course.
- Line managers have training guidelines for employees.
- Course development uses instructional design techniques.
- Measurements exist to ensure learning, retention, and application of lessons.
- Use of cost-effective delivery systems is maximized.

- A system exists to monitor employee completions.
- Training cost is planned and controlled.

This phase should be broken up into two or three milestones to demonstrate progress and, at the same time, encourage progress. Here are three sample milestones:

- Pilot curricula implemented
- One-third of curricula implemented
- Two-thirds of curricula implemented

Phase 5: Structured education. In this phase, the lessons described in this book have been implemented. The job, of course, is never finished because new education methods will constantly be developed. For example, expert systems will play a major role in future education systems. Only organizations that have implemented structured education will benefit from future advances in technology and methodology. Those organizations will have the potential to achieve and sustain a major competitive advantage through lower labor costs and higher productivity.

How does the five-phase management system to measure the progress of moving from unstructured to structured education work in practice? Without a road map like the "Systems Approach To Education" or a measurement system to assess progress, it took IBM 15 years to make the progress that is now possible in five years. The lessons in this book permit an organization to increase dramatically the rate of implementation of structured education.

IBM is now in phase 4 in almost every area of education (a few functions within the company have already reached phase 5). Arthur Andersen & Co. is one of the very few organizations in the country that has fully implemented phase 5. One reason IBM has been able to make so much progress is the review system that was described in Chapter 9. The annual review by the management committee on the health of education has brought a focus on education that mandates progress. It is important to remember, however, that progress requires more than management focus. The management system must support a vision like that embodied in IBM's systems approach to education.

Chapter 3 through 10 have described the building blocks of programs and decisions necessary to raise education's quality and contain its costs. It is important to remember that this system to manage change in education is not unique to IBM and other large companies. The lessons in this book also work within intermediate-size companies, government agencies and not-for-profit organizations.

PART 3 ///

TRANSFERRING THE LESSONS FOR RESTRUCTURING EDUCATION

11 ///

Applying the Lessons to Primary and Secondary Education

The federal government produces thousands of reports every year. Only a few have a real impact on the nation, but a report that sounded an alarm on education has now been referred to regularly for over five years. Rarely does a single report make such a strong impression on such a large part of our society.

In 1983, the National Commission on Excellence in Education presented a report on the quality of education in America to then Secretary of Education T. H. Bell. The report was called *A Nation at Risk: The Imperative for Education Reform.* The commission was created in 1981 as a result of the secretary's concern about "the widespread public perception that something is seriously remiss in our education system." The report's most famous passage reads:

> We report to the American people that while we can take justifiable pride in what our schools and colleges have historically accomplished and contributed to the United States and the well-being of its people, the education foundations of our society are presently being eroded by a rising tide of mediocrity that threatens our very future as a Nation and a people. What was unimaginable a generation ago has begun to occur—others are matching and surpassing our education attainments. If an unfriendly foreign power had attempted to impose on America the

153

mediocre education performance that exists today, we might well have viewed it as an act of war. As it stands, we have allowed this to happen to ourselves.

Then the report listed indicators of the problems.

- International comparisons of student achievement reveal that on 19 academic tests American students were never first or second and, in comparison with other industrial nations, were last seven times.
- Some 23 million American adults are functionally illiterate by the simplest tests of everyday reading, writing, and comprehension.
- About 13 percent of all 17-year-olds in the United States can be considered functionally illiterate. Functional illiteracy among minority youth may run as high as 40 percent.
- Average achievement of high school students on most standardized tests is now lower than 26 years ago, when Sputnik was launched.
- College Board achievement tests also reveal consistent declines in recent years in such subjects as physics and English.
- There was a steady decline in science achievement scores of U.S. 17-year-olds as measured by national assessments of science in 1969, 1973, and 1977.
- Between 1975 and 1980, remedial mathematics courses in public four-year colleges increased by 72 percent and now constitute one-quarter of all mathematics courses taught in those institutions.
- The average graduate of our schools and colleges today is not as well-educated as the average graduate of 25 or 35 years ago, when a much smaller proportion of our population completed high school and college.

On the personal level, the student, the parent, and the caring teacher all perceive that a basic promise is not being kept. More and more young people emerge from high school ready neither for college nor for work. This predicament becomes more acute as the knowledge base continues its rapid expansion, the number of traditional jobs shrink, and new jobs demand greater sophistication and preparation.

The report went on to say

On a broader scale, we sense that this undertone of frustration has significant political implications, for it cuts across ages, generations, races, and political and economic groups. We have come to understand that the public will demand that educational and political leaders act forcefully and effectively on these issues. Indeed, such demands have already appeared and could well become a unifying national preoccupation.

This report generated several years of education reform and helped to bring a focus on education in a way that no other report has ever done. Some people refer to the impact of the report as the "first wave" of education reform to sweep across the nation's public schools.

In spite of the report's strong language and the overpowering evidence it presented showing a clear decline in the quality of education in the United States, some educators would like you to believe that the schools are about the same as they were 25 to 40 years ago. They claim the problem is one of raising the school systems to a new level of performance demanded by the global economy, which requires our workers to compete with workers of many countries. Fortunately, this argument has not slowed efforts to improve our school systems, which, on average, are not as good as they were years ago.

THE RESULTS OF FIVE YEARS OF REFORM

The vast majority of states have appointed education task forces. Most have increased the starting salaries of teachers as well as the overall compensation connected with the salary scale. In fact, education spending rose $56 billion, or 43.4 percent, during the past few years. Teachers' pay rose 46.8 percent. Since 1983, 37 states have considered lengthening the school year, but only nine have done so. Most states have raised high-school graduation requirements. SAT scores have risen 16 points (out of a possible 1600), ending a long downward slide. One-fourth of the schools have strengthened homework policies. Teacher standards have been raised.

Texas has one of the most visible reform programs, which has been spearheaded by entrepreneur H. Ross Perot and supported by Governor Mark White. They helped to push through the most sweeping school overhaul in the state's 150-year history. The most famous of Texas's reforms is the so-called "no-pass, no play" regulation that bars students who fail even one course from participating in any sports or other extracurricular activities for six weeks. This highly controversial rule has overshadowed many other more important reforms, but it has set a tone. Gone are the days when students could take off several weeks from school to prepare for livestock shows or other events.

Classes in Texas schools are smaller now. Teachers are paid much better, but many resent the tests of their subject-matter competency that they have been forced to take. The vast majority of teachers (99.1 percent) has passed the test, but they complain about the suspicion they feel is embodied in the test that they are not competent in the subjects they teach. The teachers also resent the need to teach students certain lessons covered on statewide tests.

A statewide minimum passing grade of 70 has been imposed on all courses. The old system of promoting students automatically from grade to grade after each year in school has been stopped. Credit is denied in any course for which a student has more than five unexcused absences per semester.

A statewide system of on-the-job appraisal has been established for all teachers and administrators. Four times a year, an evaluator spends a full class-period observing each teacher; the evaluator completes a critique sheet with 54 items. Teachers who have been evaluating performance and giving out grades for years, now find themselves in the unusual and sometimes uncomfortable position of being evaluated themselves.

The Texas reforms are much more aggressive than those instituted by most states. At the time the reforms were approved, Texas ranked 47th out of 50 states on SAT scores. The sweeping reforms were thought essential to bring change to a state with such a low education ranking.

Based on the reforms of the 1980s, how much better will the results of education be? Unfortunately, few quality measurements are in place with which to evaluate the results of education reform. One measurement that is available, however, is that of the cost of education. The reforms and the increase in payroll have cost billions of dollars. The cost of existing education systems has dramatically increased in the 1980s.

Teachers' pay increases have been the largest factor in the rising education cost. At the end of the 1988 school year, the average salary for the nation's 2.3 million public school teachers was $29,573. The pay raises are exceeding the cost of inflation. Averaged nationally, the cost of educating each student from kindergarten through 12th grade is just under $4,000 a year. William Bennett, the controversial Secretary of Education from 1985 to 1988, accused the schools and the nation's largest teachers union of backsliding on reforms and of holding up progress by asking for "gobs and gobs" of new money. He said, "The American people have paid and paid dearly for education, but as yet they have not been given their money's worth."

When you take another look at dropout rates, illiteracy rates, and the number of people who cannot hold a minimum-wage job, you realize that school reform must continue. In the 1990s, there must be a second phase of school reform. The second phase of school reform must be based on measurable improvements in education. The lessons learned within employee education can be a big assist to this second phase of school reform, which will really design the school systems for the 21st century. The second phase of school reform must emphasize both an increase in quality and the containment of costs. Throwing money at education is not going to solve the problems that exist today. The first phase of education reform left the basic education systems intact. The reform movement has been modest up to now. Change has been more symbolic than substantive.

WHAT DO WE LEARN FROM THE STUDIES AND REPORTS?

As I stated in the introduction, more than 300 reports have been issued by the various task forces and study groups that have focused on our school systems. One of the best of these reports was published by the Committee for Economic Development and was entitled, *Investing in Our Children: Business and the Public Schools.* The six points that follow summarize how education in the business world is related to education in the public schools.

- The most important investment this nation can make is in its children. When public schools are successful, they become a national treasure. They can instruct and inspire our young people. They can give life to local communities, contributing to their economic growth and social well-being. They can pave the road to employment, greater opportunity, and more productive lives. In our pluralistic democracy, the schools can forge a common culture while respecting diversity. But for all these possibilities, many of our schools stand accused of failing the nation's children and leaving the economy vulnerable to better educated and more highly trained international competitors.
- Business should make a long-term commitment to support the public schools. Companies should provide policy and project support and targeted funding, with the *expectation that the schools will improve their performance.* But business should not be expected to provide general funding for education beyond the taxes it pays to the community. The schools are the central public institution for the development of human resources. Tomorrow's work force is in today's classroom; the skills that these students develop and the attitudes toward work that they acquire will help determine the performance of our businesses and the course of our society in the twenty-first century.
- Public education's most important task is to ensure that all school children are grounded in basic academic and behavioral skills. Our school system should prepare youngsters for responsible citizenship and

should impart skills and attributes that will enable them to succeed in productive employment or higher education. Business, in general, is not interested in narrow vocationalism. It prefers a curriculum that stresses literacy and mathematical and problem-solving skills. Such a curriculum should emphasize learning how to learn and adapting to change. The schools should also teach and reward self-discipline, reliability, teamwork, acceptance of responsibility, and respect for the rights of others.

- A high school diploma should indicate that a student has met or exceeded an established standard of achievement, and we urge all states to establish a minimum standard of performance for awarding a diploma. We also endorse honors diplomas to signify superior accomplishment.
- We recommend enhancing and strengthening the professional roles of teachers, increasing their ability and opportunity to exercise judgement and make decisions, raising their salaries, and upgrading their working conditions. None of these improvements can be made without strengthening school management and leadership. In sum, we are calling for nothing less than a revolution in the role of the teacher and the management of the schools.

I agree with all these fundamental statements on education. The big, basic question is, "How do we achieve all the hopes and expectations that people have for our school systems?" Unfortunately, the question has never been answered very well. Most people do not see the similarities in the processes of education that apply within employee education and the elementary and secondary education system. The lessons learned in the world of employee education will, however, come to have a major impact on the primary and secondary education systems in the United States. This chapter is devoted to showing how some of the lessons in Chapters 3 through 9 apply to primary and secondary schools.

Government agencies, not-for-profit organizations, and profit-making companies are the consumers of the graduates from our public and private schools. As these organizations become more knowledgeable about successful employee education methods, they will be much more demanding on the school systems who provide their future employees. Many business managers and executives are members of school boards and education task forces. As they become aware of how education should be managed they will become much more active members.

Employers will eventually bring great pressure on the government and the education systems to improve the quality of future employees. This improvement must not only be in basic skills such as reading, writing, and mathematics, but also in good work habits and accept-able behavior. People who graduate from high school must be reliable, adult citizens who can earn a living. The number of entrance exami-nations and more thorough reviews of academic records will increase for people seeking employment because the cost of recruiting an un-qualified or poorly trained employee is too great. Companies want to avoid remedial training expenses, currently estimated to be in the hundreds of millions of dollars.

In 1986, the Business Roundtable performed a study of the attitudes toward American education of 118 large companies. The survey's purpose was to define the views of American business on the quality of primary and secondary education systems. The questionnaire asked businesses to evaluate the products of our education system—the high school graduates entering the labor force. Here are a few comments from the executive summary:

- American businesses are disappointed in the general quality of high school graduates, in their preparation for the world of work, and in their education for entering the labor force.
- More than a third of American businesses have difficulty trying to recruit well-educated employees.
- American businesses agree that the fundamental problems in the pri-mary and secondary education systems are: failure to teach about the world of work (85%); insufficient attention to the basics (82%); failure to provide career counseling (76%); and school board policies which fail to emphasize strong curricula (68%).
- The competencies which will be more important in the future are the ones allowing employees to adapt to changing demands and to be innovative. Close behind are the basics of reading, writing, and mathematics.
- American business very eagerly endorses a wide range of active roles for itself to improve the education quality.

The number one recommendation of the most recent study by the Business Roundtable is to initiate no further studies on education, but to use the research already conducted. The Business Roundtable continues to provide a sustained commitment to education including the school/business partnerships at the state and local level.

HOW IS BUSINESS TRYING TO HELP EDUCATION?

The Business Roundtable companies conducted another survey of 104 companies to determine what education initiatives were being sponsored by various businesses. They learned about hundreds of such programs. Here are a few examples:

- "Adopt-A-School" programs
- Employee volunteer programs
- Donation of classroom materials and equipment
- Computer projects
- Math, science, and energy programs
- Basic skills development
- Career exploration
- Business and economic education
- Special education programs
- Minority-student programs
- Summer youth programs
- Work-experience programs
- Curriculum development and revitalization
- Teacher internships and training
- Foundations
- Scholarship and recognition programs
- Conference sponsorships

Under the auspices of the Committee for Economic Development, Marsha Levine and Roberta Trachtman wrote a book entitled *American Business and the Public School,* which includes case studies of corporate involvement in public education. The case studies show how important it is for top management to be involved for there to be a real impact on the school systems. As Levine and Trachtman write, "Business/school collaboration has become a trendy piece of the education reform movement."

The National Alliance For Business is yet another organization that has encouraged the support of education by the major companies of our country. In fact, almost every major business organization—the Chamber of Commerce, the Conference Board, and others—is supporting the need to raise the quality of education.

Business is trying to help improve the quality of education in two fundamental ways. First, businesses have spent millions in an attempt to enhance the current school systems using the traditional methods of instruction. Second, a few companies are trying to develop new processes for education because a few business executives know that schools must be restructured for there to be any major measurable improvement in the performance of education systems.

PARTNERSHIP TO IMPROVE EXISTING EDUCATION SYSTEMS

Years ago, almost every home in America had someone in school. The partnership of education with parents, grandparents, and students covered a majority of households. Today, only a minority of homes has a direct relationship with the schools. There is therefore a need for a new partnership.

Business leaders have been serving on school boards from the very beginning of the public school system. Executives are now more active than ever because they realize the competence of their workers is directly dependent upon the success of the primary and secondary schools. With a predicted labor shortage and a competitive marketplace already in existence, American business leaders want to help education improve in every way possible.

At the same time, education leaders have shifted from a hands-off attitude to one of gratitude toward the business community because of the part is has played in fending off acute funding shortages and widespread criticisms. Educators also feel that many positive aspects of their education programs are not receiving adequate recognition, a problem that having a partnership with business can help to fix.

Partnerships usually have several objectives:

- Recognize teachers and help to keep them current in their field of study
- Motivate students to greater academic achievement
- Encourage students to learn about citizenship and the responsibilities of being a productive adult
- Assist students to enter the job market or achieve acceptance to institutions of higher education.

Normally, the partnerships do not become involved in curriculum reviews, content definition of courses, or in the process of education. These areas are viewed as off-limits to the business community.

The Atlanta Partnership of Business and Education was founded in 1981, before the "Nation At Risk" alarm was sounded. The organization's overall goal is "to improve the quality of life for the people of our area by improving their educational attainment level." The partnership's charter makes three major points:

- *Education* must be our number one national priority.
- *Quality* must be our national watchword.
- *Everyone* has a role to play.

One interesting program sponsored by the Atlanta Partnership is the Superintendent/Deans' Breakfast Club, which brings together the superintendent of the Atlanta public schools and the deans of the various schools and colleges of education in the Atlanta area. This group meets for one to two hours each month.

The Atlanta Partnership started with 150 members and four major programs: Adopt-A-School, affirmative action job placement, advisement (employees impart personal experience on the job to enhance students' know-how or practical knowledge), and student tutorial programs. By 1985, the Atlanta Partnership had helped the Georgia General Assembly pass the Quality Basic Education (QBE) Act, the most sweeping (and most expensive) piece of legislation ever to be passed in Georgia. The bill passed without a single dissenting vote in either house. The partnership now includes more than 350 companies and has helped bring great sums of new money to education.

The Boston Compact is probably the most famous of the business/education partnerships. In 1982, again before the "Nation At Risk" report, the labor, education, and business communities started to work together to improve the quality of education available to Boston students. The unique part of the Boston Compact's program has been to link the improvement of school performance to job opportunities. The Boston Compact has found thousands of summer jobs for young people and placed large numbers of high-school graduates in full-time jobs. At the same time, the partnership has helped improve reading and mathematics scores as well as attendance. The Boston Compact has invested $2 million in dropout prevention. The National Alliance of Business funded a demonstration project for the Boston Compact, which helped move this model to other cities and states. Minnesota, Cincinnati, Indianapolis, Washington, D.C., Memphis, Louisville, Seattle, and San Diego are other states and cities that have business/education partnerships.

RESULTS OF BUSINESS/EDUCATION PARTNERSHIPS

The overall results of business/education partnerships have been positive. Teachers and principals like the recognition that business has given education. Business leaders feel a real sense of accomplishment based on a steady stream of reports that provide positive feedback on the various programs. Most of these measurements are quantitative. Victory is being claimed on the basis of the number of schools adopted, the number of students tutored, the number of presentations made by business people, the number of students attending career day, and so on. Unfortunately, this declaration of victory is premature. The large number of dropouts remains. Too many students who graduate from high school continue to be unemployable because of a lack of skills and knowledge. "The reform movement has been most successful with those students who need it the least," says Ernest Boyer, president of the Carnegie Foundation for the Advancement of Teaching. For inner-city students, little has changed. The bottom half of the class has not improved, according to many educators. So far, most of the motivation for reform has come from governors, legislators, and business concerned about a shrinking pool of qualified workers. The reform movement has not reached into the classroom to change the process of learning. If business, government, and education were to receive their grades after five years of school reform, the marks might read:

A, for increasing the funding to education

B, for stopping the decline in quality

C, for instituting measurements on performance and accountability

D, for improving the process of education

WILL IMPROVED MANAGEMENT FIX THE PROBLEMS?

Most of the problems faced by primary and secondary schools do not apply to wealthy suburban schools, which, despite the sharp words usually traded at the annual budget event, have above-average budgets. Suburban parents support good schools and encourage their children to do well. Most of the students are motivated. Attracting qualified teachers to these schools is quite easy. Maybe the bottom fourth of the class needs help, but most of the students go on to college. Those that do not are well qualified to obtain jobs. Unfortunately, these schools represent a small minority of the more than 15,000 school districts in the country.

Most school districts are struggling to attract new teachers as well as to retain their experienced teachers. Job satisfaction and morale is low among the professional staff. The dropout rate is an embarrassment. A majority of students appear to dislike school. This environment presents one of the great challenges of management.

School superintendents and principals who are weak managers foster an environment in which horror stories like the following occur:

A new woman left a private-sector job to become a primary school teacher. She was treated like a person in the unemployment line when she applied for the job. Her principal never properly introduced her to the support staff or to her fellow teachers. The other teachers made her feel completely unwelcome. Her classroom did not have the proper furniture. She received her books and course materials two weeks after the class started. On the first day of class, she had no curriculum guides, no class lists, no operating procedures. Attendance averaged about 60 percent. Her fourth-grade students could not understand her lessons because they could barely read or write. She described the school as "not the worst, but by no means one of the best." Needless to say, she gave up her teaching career. The administrators in this situation were filling time until retirement. There is little hope for a school system with weak management.

On the other hand, some school systems have outstanding administrators. One of my most impressive meetings was with the school superintendent and his assistant superintendents in Dade County, Florida, which includes the city of Miami. At one time, the schools in this district were no better than most inner-city schools. Today, after several outstanding administrators, the school system is considered one of the best in our country. This transformation has taken great creativity and leadership. The management team in Dade County has tried *many* of the reforms instituted in cities around the country. A working partnership has been built between the teachers' union and the administrators. This has been helped by a new salary program that averages 28 percent increases over the next three years, with the outstanding teachers earning as much as $64,000. A pilot project to test a career ladder has been set in motion. Teachers and principals are working together to improve the schools. Parents are becoming more involved in the support of their schools. New measurement systems clearly identify the outstanding schools, the average schools, and the below-average schools. Buildings are being renovated, and new faculty workrooms and lounges are being built. The school-district leader, Joseph Fernandez, is rated as one of the most creative superintendents in the country by Albert Shanker, president of the American Federation of Teachers.

The former superintendent of Dade County, Leonard Britton, is now the chief educator in Los Angeles. Already he has issued a report with 612 recommendations for improving Los Angeles schools. The report, 409 pages long and two years in the making, is the work of 226 school administrators, teachers, staff members, parents, students, and community workers. It will be interesting to see if the nation's second-largest school system can show a turnaround like that made by Dade County. That would begin to put some real peer pressure on other large city school systems!

Rochester, New York, is another city that is trying to empower teachers with a more decentralized system and major wage increases. Good management policies and leadership are already making a difference.

As I look back on the meetings I have had with the leaders of some of the best-managed school systems, I notice one area that needs more attention. That is the measurement of learning within each subject area. Teachers' performance and accountability in improving the process of learning has yet to be achieved. There is no doubt that students learn more in a well-managed school, but we appear to be a long way from having almost all the students liking and doing well in school. There is no talk about *mastery* of the lessons. The dropout rate remains high. The bottom half of the class has many "at risk" students.

THE CASE FOR RESTRUCTURING SCHOOLS

Business executives and educators too often accept the current process of education with an attitude of resignation. Too often, teachers and administrators will not allow changes in the classroom. When business executives compare the process of education in employee education to the process of education in the public schools they will not be satisfied with current methods. As costs continue to climb at an accelerated rate and quality measurements creep up by only a few percentage points, many penetrating questions will be raised. The case for restructuring the schools will be sounded again and again.

David Kearns, the CEO of Xerox, in his book *Winning the Brain Race*, writes,

> Public education in this country is in crisis. America's public schools graduate 700,000 functionally illiterate students every year, and 700,000 more drop out. Four out of five young adults in a recent survey could not summarize the main point of a newspaper article, or read a bus schedule, or figure their change from a restaurant bill. At a time when our pre-eminent role in the world economy is in jeopardy, there are few social problems more telling in their urgency. Public education has put this country at a terrible competitive disadvantage. The task before us is the restructuring of our entire public education system. I don't mean tinkering.

I don't mean piecemeal changes or even well-intentional reforms. I mean the total restructuring of our schools.

To date, however, the business community has treated the schools with kid gloves. On the positive side of the ledger, that reflects a deep and abiding commitment to public education that the business community shares. On the negative side, however, it spares the schools. It permits them to think that incremental change will be enough. It will not.

How will this restructuring take place? For years, school administrators and school boards have debated the question, "Should high school students be required to take a personal typing class?" Most schools offer an elective personal typing course. The justification is that future college students need to be able to type term papers. There should be no debate in today's world. Every high school graduate needs keyboard skills. In the future, very few people will have jobs that do not demand that some tasks be performed on a computer terminal. Leaving high school today without keyboard skills makes a potential worker less qualified. Business and government leaders should insist on this basic skill. Eventually, they may go further and demand that students take a computer literacy course in order to graduate from high school. In 1987, Senator Christopher J. Dodd of Connecticut said, "We must shed the national mindset that looks upon computers as fancy frills in our education system. They are the pencils and paper of the 21st century."

Traditional educators will claim they cannot afford such expensive classes. But if the school system does not teach basic skills and knowledge, the business community and government agencies will have employee-education budgets that increase every year. Billions of dollars are being spent in the current school systems, and that investment must be made to yield qualified workers and productive citizens. Major new goals must be established for the second wave of school reform to warrant the huge investment of incremental funds that will be spent on education in the 1990s. The following goals show how high we should reach to justify the billions of dollars that will surely be expended.

1. Drastically reduce the dropout rate from the high 20s to only a few percent.
2. Stop the graduation of students who are unemployable. High school graduates must have a basic set of skills and knowledge.

3. Raise the performance of American students so that they are at least first or second in the world in every major academic competition.

4. Achieve mastery of the lessons so that the vast majority of students obtain an A or B as a course grade.

5. Through opinion surveys, measure the attitude of students and have the vast majority liking school.

6. Achieve a breakthrough in job satisfaction for experienced teachers through working conditions, improved facilities, and adequate salaries.

7. Based on the above six objectives, develop programs that attract outstanding people to the teaching profession.

Are these goals an impossible dream? To justify the rapid increases in cost during the 1980s, which will continue into the 1990s, we should be satisfied with nothing less than these objectives. A dramatic increase must occur in the quality of education. Schools must be restructured to improve the process of education. The public and the world of education need to see a vision based on these objectives.

In an article entitled "Saving One High School," which appeared in the May 2, 1988, issue of *Newsweek,* reporter Timothy Noah describes Orangeburg-Wilkinson High School in South Carolina. He calls it a success story of the education-reform movement. The 2,000 students who attend this semirural high school are not wealthy. Seventy-five percent qualify for federal reduced-price or free lunches. The school's past performance was not distinguished. It had a poor academic record and more than its share of discipline problems. Some of the problems were rooted in a history of racial tension. Students smoked marijuana openly on campus. English classes were often devoted to such student-council activities as building homecoming floats.

A new building was built in 1984. A new principal was hired. Teacher salaries have been raised from an average of $17,000 in 1984 to $25,000 in 1988, and some outstanding teachers are also eligible for merit bonuses. Parents are involved with the school. The school has installed several computer labs. Yes, they are using technology in the process of education. In fact, the school has one computer for every ten students and hopes to add more. Measurements have been installed to show the rate of improvement. The Orangeburg-Wilkinson High School has won South Carolina's School

Incentive Reward Program twice in the last four years. Clearly, it takes good management, restructuring, and a new process of education for major increases in performance to occur.

HOW WILL A DRAMATIC INCREASE IN QUALITY COME ABOUT?

The plan of action for improving education cannot be a timid set of cosmetic changes. It must be a bold set of programs. The effort to bring fundamental change to our school systems will be like building the nationwide expressway system we all enjoy driving on today. Years ago, each community had a number of people who resisted every mile of the new expressways. Today, even though a few remaining links have not yet been built because of local resistance, we have an impressive highway system. Moving away from the old school systems will be like moving away from the old two-lane highways with all their curves and stoplights. The following eight-step plan of action will lead to major improvements to our public schools.

Step 1: Establish a second National Commission on Excellence in Education

In 1981-1983, the first commission gained attention and created interest in the need for change in our school systems. The new President, the new Congress, and the new Secretary of Education that have taken office in 1989 have an opportunity to capitalize on the public sentiment for an improved education system. They should seize this opportunity and appoint a second commission built on a partnership of education, business, and government. The first commission defined the problems. The second commission should work in the early 1990s on solutions to improve the process of education. The commission should be charged with the responsibility to draw up the long-range plan. It should create and communicate the vision of a much improved education system.

Step 2: Establish goals, strategies, and measurements

Goals that state where this country wants to be in education by the late 1990s should be established. Strategies and plans are required to make progress toward our goals. Milestones need to be established so that major steps along the journey to the goals can be determined, and to tell us whether our action programs are successful. For example, if one goal is to reach a dropout rate of less than 5 percent by the year 2000, a set of interim milestones should be established for the years 1990–2000. Measurements are required to determine how effective courses are. (We are not talking about testing kindergarten children to see if they are qualified for first grade.) Nor should the tests hold back large numbers of students. If that happens, something is wrong with the process of education.

Step 3: Design and develop curricula of courses

In this step, a basic question needs to be answered: What do you want the students to know and to be able to do at the end of twelve years of education? Georgia legislators, in this Quality Basic Education (QBE) program, agreed on 76 competencies. Again, there are no major surprises on the list.

Once basic competencies have been identified, instructional designers would use the design techniques that have been developed and practiced in employee education to determine course objectives and major learning points for the subjects that have been agreed upon by the new national commission. As the courses are designed, measurements and exercises should be built into the course materials. Course development companies and publishing companies working with graduate schools of education would be asked to develop new courses. Local school systems could continue to select which of the available courses would be used in their school system. However, any course for a given subject (e.g., general science) would be taught toward achieving a single set of objectives and to cover the basic learning points. Some people think central curriculum planning is a radical idea, but even today, books are published on the assumption that they can be used by any school system in the country. There is the old story that an educator traveled across the country, stopping in a different school each day, and never missed a lesson. The lessons taught in our school systems must be similar or people could not move their children from one community to another. High school graduates could not apply to various colleges across the country and employees could not be transfered to various parts of the country.

Step 3 should also raise the quality of books and other course materials. The curriculum that former secretary Bennett put forward in December 1987 looked almost identical to the curriculum that I had while attending an inner-city school 40 years earlier. A great deal of debate would surround course content, but agreement would not be an impossible task.

Step 4: Pilot test four or five model schools

Step four is the big challenge that will result in the major changes. The Commission On Excellence In Education should establish four or five pilot schools that will not be inhibited by current teaching or administrative methods. Each pilot school would be run by a partnership consisting of a leading school of education, book publishers, education development companies, and companies that provide software systems, networks, computers, and personal computers designed for education. The pilot school must be an existing school, which a city would make available for several years. Its students should be neither the best nor the worst. The partnership would try new ideas and programs but at the same time would ensure that the students would complete normal academic achievements during the pilot test (tutors may be necessary if one or another of the programs does not succeed).

Each pilot school would be free to use as much technology or as little technology as its administrators feel is required. The role of a teacher could be changed dramatically or it might be similar to the current practice. Class periods could be 30 minutes or several hours long. School buildings could be remodeled, but new buildings and major modifications would raise the final cost of the program and therefore would have to be carefully justified. The local school administrators and the participating school of education would be responsible for ensuring that the new programs are educationally sound.

The intent of the pilot program would be to encourage maximum creativity in designing a future school in order to achieve the most significant gain possible in learning and skill-building. When the five pilot schools have completed their research and development, the best of the five should be identified and its program applied to two or three systems. At this point, local school boards are free to continue business as usual, or to phase-in one of the new education systems (or selected aspects of that system).

Federal and/or state government would invest a few million dollars a year in each model school as part of the partnership. The business partner could invest additional funds and equipment. Remember, the objectives are to raise the education quality and contain costs. Expensive solutions are not going to sell in the public education marketplace, so creating expensive, nonmarketable solutions would be a waste of time and money.

No matter which decision on instituting new learning systems is made, the local school board, administration, and teaching staff would be required to achieve new standards in education based on the six major objectives described earlier. New measurements and standards are the key factor in the management of change. If there are no new standards, business as usual will go on in spite of education reforms. One reason that so few new education programs are successful is the lack of measurements to evaluate the new system against the old. For example, if the new standard is a 5 percent dropout rate rather than 30 percent, there must be changes in the system to achieve the new standards.

Remember, in business, it is essential that all students be successful. The objective is for everyone to master the lessons. Employee educators do not want 10 percent A students, 20 percent B students, 40 percent C students, 20 percent D students, and 10 percent F students. The normal "bell curve" is unacceptable in employee education—as it should also be in public school education. If mastery of lessons is possible after 18 years of age by nearly all, maybe 90% of all students could be A and B students in grammar school and high school. Perhaps this could be one of the new standards set by the commission. If we are investing in new methods, new technology, and new courses, we must have dramatic improvements in the performance of education.

Is all this just a wild idea? Not at all, as this example of a school that has already been restructured will show. Dustin H. Heuston is a career educator who holds a doctorate in English and American Literature from New York University. He is the founder and chairman of the WICAT company, which develops courseware for new education systems that rely on personal tutoring systems as well as teachers. Heuston's message is very simple. No amount of money will improve the current American education system. He points out that between 1950 and 1975, the share of the U.S. gross national product spent on education rose from 3.4 percent to 7.4 percent. In the 1980s, the growth of this cost accelerated beyond the rate of the previous 25-year period. During this period, with few exceptions, student performance (as measured by standardized tests) has declined.

In the early 1980s, Heuston formed a nonprofit institute, Waterford School, to test his theories and courses on the first twelve grades. Located in Orem, Utah, the research school has over 400 students in 12 grades. Heuston's investment may eventually reach $100 million over a ten-year period. Courses that have been developed at the Waterford School are already in use in 350 schools around the country, with about 150,000 students nationwide working with computer courses designed by Waterford educators. After five years of intensive analysis, Waterford moved from standardized test scores that averaged in the 67th percentile to scores in the 91st percentile. That is a dramatic change. The students use computers about one hour a day. Not everyone will agree with Heuston's research or methods, but he has proved that taking a systems approach to education in the primary and secondary grades can lead to the same breakthroughs as in the business world.

Heuston is not alone among educators seriously engaged in restructuring education in the United States. "Writing to Read," an instructional program using personal tutoring systems, has come a long way since a retiree in Stuart, Florida, approached IBM several years ago and asked for the loan of some typewriters. Dr. John Henry Martin, teacher, principal, superintendent, professor, and author, was fascinated with the process of how children learn. Frustrated by children's difficulties in coping with the complexities of the English language and exasperated by the large number of students who reach advanced grades without being able to read or write, Martin invented a system in which children learn to read by first learning to write. The Educational Testing Service at Princeton, New Jersey, after an extensive two-year evaluation, has concluded that "Writing to Read" is an effective educational program. The testing of the course material before implementation is, in itself, a major new approach to education. Over a million students have so far been touched by this program.

One of Martin's backers at IBM has been Jim Dezell, who manages the development of advanced education systems for grades K through 12. Dezell believes that a technology-based learning environment is better than traditional instruction because it is risk-free from the student's perspective even though frequent measurements are built into programs in the form of exercises on the computer. There are no failures and no red-pencil marks. There is no labeling of students—no slow group or fast group. The new systems foster learning through discovery, which is the best of all teaching methods for motivating students to learn. Each child becomes responsible for his or her own learning, which is the empowering element that improves self-esteem. There are many more educators like Dr. Heuston, Dr. Martin, and Mr. Dezell who could be working on schoolwide solutions in pilot schools such as those proposed in step 4.

It is interesting to note that these three educators are working on the *process of education.* They are using systematic methods for course development, new quality measurements, and new technology to improve the process of education. They are willing to change almost anything to improve the level of learning while containing costs at the same time. They are not intimidated by the words "personal computer." In fact, they are using the personal computer as a personal tutoring system, which is one of the great breakthroughs in education.

Every educator knows that students learn faster and better if they have a personal tutor. No school system can afford to hire a $25,000–$30,000 teacher as a personal tutor for each child, but a $1,000 computer *can* serve that role. The $1,000 computer will work as many hours as needed over a period of five to ten years, so the "tutor" will end up costing a couple of hundred dollars per student, which would represent about a 5 percent increase in the cost of education per student assuming that there are no savings from reallocation of resources and cost avoidance. But there would be such savings if a school were significantly restructured. For example, putting one more student in each class would save $5 billion per year nationwide. Yet many educators are waiting for the price of a personal computer to go as low as the price of a textbook ($25.00!) before they will consider such a different approach to teaching and learning.

Even business executives who have the courage to call for a complete restructuring of education are careful to avoid talking about technology or personal computers. The outstanding *Investing in Our Children*, by the Committee for Economic Development, has over 100 pages of advice on how to improve education but only this one paragraph on the use of advanced technology:

> The needs of education reform are sweeping. Therefore, this report does not deal in depth with such critical issues as the role of technology in education's future. We do, however, strongly endorse the need for expanded education research and data collection in these and other areas and better application of research findings.

That is not a bold approach to restructuring education. It is a timid statement. Business must be willing to come to grips with the tough and controversial issues if it is going to have an impact on education. In their book *Winning the Brain Race*, Dave Kearns and Denis Doyle have the courage to write:

> Fine schools for the future are not the same as fine schools for the past. We do not need more of the same incremental change. We need radical change, transforming change. As human capital intensive organizations, they [corporations] are not afraid to replace labor with capital when appropriate. Indeed, the public schools, if they are to survive and prosper, must take a page from the high tech book.

Can you imagine talking to the airline industry or the banks or insurance companies 25 years ago and being afraid to discuss the role of computers in their industry? Yet business executives and government leaders are almost afraid to discuss technology with leaders of the education industry. There are even some articles that imply that teachers cannot learn how to use computers, which is ridiculous because every level of worker today uses a keyboard and a computer. Some people are calling education programs like Writing to Read "learning systems," because they have the following characteristics:

1. The programs ensure that students will learn the key lessons. They will master the subject and obtain the skills.

2. Success at learning builds self-esteem of the student. Their self-confidence is enhanced.

3. Course material is self-paced and the content is motivational. Students enjoy learning.

4. Students work at learning. They understand the lessons by thinking, not just remembering facts.

5. Teachers manage the learning process that includes high quality course materials, personal tutoring and classroom teaching.

Step 5: Develop a plan to fund new education systems

The national interstate highway system became a reality only when federal, state, and local governments agreed on who would select contractors and who would pay the bills. Local school boards must take part in the decisions on future school systems, but they cannot fund all the new systems. Local governments fund about 43 percent of current education systems; state governments fund almost 50 percent, and the federal government less than 10 percent.

One way to parcel out responsibility for funding a new system might be to have the federal government fund the research and development. Education course development companies and publishers could continue to fund new course development, especially if they are building courses for national or state standards. State governments might fund new equipment and building modifications. Local governments would continue to control overall budgets and personnel as well as the content of the courses.

Step 6: Establish job placement as a measurement of effectiveness

Most high schools are concerned about getting their bright students into colleges and universities. Other than that, they don't seem to feel responsible for the students after graduation. In the future, there should be new standards to measure the effectiveness of the school system in the placing of students in either productive jobs or schools of higher learning. Employment problems for high-school graduates have persisted since the early 1950s. A large number of youth employment and training programs have been implemented over past years to solve this problem.

One of those programs is Jobs for American Graduates (JAG). JAG was established to conduct an extensive research effort to determine whether participation in a special program significantly enhances the ability of "at risk" high school graduates to make a successful transition from school to work. After five years, JAG has operated at an annual 85 percent success rate with 23,000 students. "At risk" students are given instruction in 33 employment competency areas such as the following:

- Career planning and decision-making
- Job search and job interviewing
- Job-holding and -keeping skills
- Basic academic skills
- Leadership and personal development skills

JAG's primary objectives are to assist participants in securing employment immediately after graduation and to improve their ability to retain employment and so avoid prolonged spells of unemployment. JAG is not the only organization with successful programs for moving high-school graduates from school to productive jobs. However, JAG's success shows that this type of program is possible. Such programs should be the day-to-day responsibility of the education system, not special, independent programs.

Step 7: Implement standardized tests

Many people are afraid that the federal or state government will control the education system if tests and standards are implemented. They do not realize that standards can also ensure methods to permit local creativity. The federal government set the standards for the national highway system. The state governments administer the highways. Local governments continue to manage city roads. We need this sort of three-tier partnership of government for a successful education system as well. Many educators talk about alternative evaluation methods because they oppose standardized tests. Unfortunately, these discussions are usually about possible concepts for evaluation, with no real research behind the alternative methods suggested. (If someone does invent a better method, there is no reason it could not be adopted later on.)

Tests are measures of our progress toward our goals. States and cities should be ranked on performance. The ranking will motivate changes, which will in turn result in higher performance levels. The United States is virtually the only industrialized country lacking national academic standards. The time has come to raise the education quality by setting standards.

Step 8: Ensure decision-making by local governments

The previous seven steps should not reduce the responsibility of local school boards and local governments to provide outstanding education for their youth. More curriculum standards are needed to help the local board make good, sound decisions.

Educators are confused about how local decision-making works in business. Yes, there is a move in business toward "quality circles" and other forms of participatory management systems, but it is important to remember that employees always make their decisions within a structured management framework. For example, IBM wants local instructors and education managers to create and teach outstanding courses. To do that, IBM insists on quality measurements, instructional design techniques, and cost-effective delivery systems. Within that management framework, local educators decide to a great extent how to teach and schedule the lessons, and when the course is over, the students must be able to demonstrate they have learned the lessons and can perform the tasks that were taught. There is no "do anything you want" environment anywhere in the business world of education because education needs to be properly resourced and respected by executive management.

We really have three choices. One is to continue business as usual and so continue to see the same results that the current education systems provide. The second choice is to adopt some new education methods, courses, and learning systems that would evolve from national or state education research projects. The third choice is to adopt a *competitive voucher system*, which former president Reagan and former education secretary Bennett proposed. This system would enable parents to apply public funds to tuition at the school of their choice—public or private.

Myron Lieberman, a professor of education at Ohio University and author of *Beyond Public Education*, claims that school reform is not working and never will. Lieberman believes that parents need the power to send children to the schools that they feel will provide the best education. He believes private schools that earn a profit for their owners will be the most innovative schools in the future. He believes good education can be both affordable and profitable. If Lieberman's predictions are correct, the American public will pay twice for education—first to the local government for a failed system and second to the new private schools. This may work for high-income couples with one or two children. It is no solution for the ordinary family in the United States. On the other hand, it is instructive to note that public school teachers in cities are more than twice as likely as the public at large to enroll their children in private schools.

U.S. STUDY OF EDUCATION IN JAPAN

The eight-step plan of action outlined above may sound far-reaching and difficult to implement, but, before anyone dismisses the need for major improvements in our school systems, he or she should read a 1987 report entitled *Japanese Education Today*, by the U.S. Department of Education.

When President Reagan and then prime minister of Japan Nakasone met in 1983, one result of their discussions was an agreement that a cooperative undertaking by Japan and the United States to study education in each other's country would be worthwhile. Here are some summary facts and thoughts from the report:

Many American educators have tended to shun the "lessons" of Japanese education because they claim their culture is so different and their society is so homogeneous that it doesn't apply in America. Americans should learn from Japan's education systems because they work. They are not perfect, but the education system is one reason why Japan has the fastest growth in their standard of living and is the envy of the world for economic expansion. Listed below are some important facts.

1. Parental engagement with the education of their children, from infancy through high school, makes a difference in how much and how well the children learn. Parents are their children's first and most influential teachers. In the United States, our school systems carry a greater responsibility to prepare high school graduates for a job and a productive life, because the family support in our country is far less than in Japan.

2. Schools [in Japan] are clear about their purposes and both the children and parents are, too. Though Japanese schools attend to character

formation, physical health, and good behavior, and offer a wide variety of teams, clubs, and other extracurricular activities they nonetheless seem to remain well focused on their central function of teaching the knowledge and skills required to be productive, employed adults.

3. Expectations and standards matter, too. Children learn more when more is expected of them. The Japanese generally seem to expect a level of performance that is closer to children's true intellectual capacities than Americans ordinarily do.

4. Sound character, study values, and ethical behavior may not originate in school, but the formal education system can reinforce and nurture these qualities.

5. The needs and preferences of employers exert strong influence on the education system. Effective school-based employment services play a significant role in matching non-college bound graduates with available jobs.

6. About 8 percent of the lower secondary school curriculum [in Japan] is devoted to industrial arts and homemaking.

7. There is a strong vocational curriculum for students not going to college.

8. A major factor in the smooth transition of students from secondary school to work is an effective job referral system. The underlying goal of the system is to minimize unemployment by giving every student a chance to be employed.

SUMMARY THOUGHTS ON PUBLIC EDUCATION

The Japanese education system is not perfect, but it has achieved results far beyond the performance of the U.S. public school system. We should not try to copy the Japanese system, because we can have a better system. The good news is that the United States has an opportunity to develop an education system that would make it number one in the world. If the instructional design techniques used within employee education are applied to developing courses for kindergarten through 12th grade and technology is used to help deliver the lessons, there is no reason the United States cannot have the finest education system in the world.

Major changes, not simple cosmetic changes, are required. If we are not willing to commit ourselves to major changes, we should stop spending millions of dollars on studying public school problems. The problems are well known and well documented. Now is the time to spend our money and our creativity on the solutions for raising education's quality and containing its costs.

People ask me if I really believe that major changes will ever be implemented in the public schools. My answer is an emphatic yes. The system can be greatly improved based on methodologies and technologies that exist today. There is no need for a major new invention to achieve progress. The solutions and improvements are affordable. Politicians like to support solutions that are affordable and feasible when there is a general feeling that a system needs to improve. Government leaders, business executives and education administrators all want to make major improvements, and they are joined by parents and other taxpayers. Former president Reagan appealed to the American people to be number one in defense. The resources were allocated and America became number one—as we always do when our country agrees on a goal. I predict the new President (of the United States) will ask the American people to restore the public-school education system to its leadership position and that we shall respond.

12 ///

Applying the Lessons to the Problem of Illiteracy

Supervisors are fond of asking, "Why don't employees work as hard as they once did?" and "Why do people nowadays make so many mistakes?" One reason may be that they do not know how to read or write. Too many employees are bluffing it. They may be able to read street signs or other simple tasks, but they are unable to read and follow directions.

HOW LARGE IS THE PROBLEM?

A great debate rages concerning how to measure illiteracy. A national study in 1987 identified the following groups as functionally illiterate (those who read below the fifth-grade level):

- 10 percent of all Americans
- 85 percent of juvenile offenders
- 50 percent of the prison population
- 70 percent of the long-term unemployed
- 40 percent of adults with incomes of less than $5,000 per year

The National Alliance of Business report cited earlier states, "Compounding the national problem is the 29% of annual high school drop outs. In the inner-city schools, the drop out rate is 50% or higher."

The cost of this problem to society is an estimated $225 billion a year in lost productivity, unrealized tax revenues, welfare, crime, unemployment, poverty, and related social ills.

The National Alliance of Business in Atlanta has issued a study called *Atlanta 2000*. It estimates that more than 30 percent of the total population cannot

- Find information in a news article
- Put in writing what they read
- Figure correct change
- Estimate cost using unit pricing
- Read and follow a map
- Use a bus schedule

As many as 23 million adult Americans are functionally illiterate, lacking basic skills beyond a fourth-grade level. Another 35 million are semi-literate, lacking skills beyond an eighth-grade level.

Some people call illiteracy the most serious problem faced by our country, exceeding the national budget and trade deficits. Others claim that illiteracy could also jeopardize our national security. Too many young people are unfit for military duty or would not be able to contribute in productive jobs during a national emergency. A few leaders are even concerned about the impact on the country's democratic ideals. An illiterate citizen, in most cases, is not fully capable of participating fully as a citizen.

WHY SHOULD WE BE CONCERNED?

In the program *At a Loss for Words: Illiterate in America*, broadcast September 3, 1986, Peter Jennings of ABC reported,

> There was a time when the United States was the most competitive industrial power on earth. In 1950, our country produced 40 percent of all the world's goods. But now the industrial base is eroding; heavy industry is leaving the country. We are a society in transition.

On the same ABC program, Gary Wuslick of LTV Steel added,

> The need for workers in the past was for their physical strength and brawn, and not for their brain. What you were expected to do when hired was to check your brain into the locker and basically take your body out on the job.

Yes, in the past, if you dropped out of school you could drop into a job that paid fairly well, which did not require basic reading, writing, or math skills. Some have pointed out that years ago many people were unable to go beyond the eighth-grade. They were not functionally illiterate. They could and did read newspapers, books, and magazines. They could read and follow directions. They had no problems handling money, deciding on a family budget, and saving within the financial systems. This, of course, is one more critical piece of evidence that our school systems have declined in quality over the last several decades.

The world is, indeed, quite different from the world faced by our parents. The Hudson Institute has produced a famous report called *Workforce 2000*, which states,

> The year 2000 will mark the end of what has been called the American century. Since 1900, the United States has become wealthy and powerful by exploiting the rapid changes taking place in technology, world trade, and the international political order.

The report goes on to say,

> If the economy is to grow rapidly and American companies are to reassert their world leadership, the education standards that have been established in the nation's schools must be raised dramatically. Put simply, students must go to school longer, study more, and pass more difficult tests covering more advanced subject matter.

A report by the U.S. Department of Labor published in March 1988 says,

> In survey after survey, employers have identified the need for workers with stronger basic skills to accomplish tasks in the workplace of today and to adapt to the workplace of tomorrow. The majority of new jobs will require some post secondary education for the first time in history. Only 27 percent of all new jobs will fall into low skill categories, compared to 40 percent of jobs today. As a consequence of smaller growth in the labor force and a diminishing pool of qualified workers, employers may face serious skills shortages not experienced since World War II. We must establish literacy as a value and weave it into the fabric of our national life.

Bill Wiggenhorn, vice president of training for Motorola, Inc., corroborates the lack of basic skills in the workplace. He has stated, "Of Motorola's U.S. employees, 5000 of them have unsatisfactory reading and mathematical skills. Another 7500 have seventh grade reading skills and fifth grade math skills. Now, new technology demands more skills." Motorola is not firing its present employees who do not meet minimum skill requirements, if, that is, they are willing to be educated. The company is sending current employees to school to raise their basic skills.

Too many people jump to the conclusion that the literacy problem is a minority problem. But over 50 percent, by some estimates, of those who are illiterate are *not* minority-group members. Not every employee is lucky enough to work for a company like Motorola, AT&T, or Ford, where remedial training is offered. The school systems must be able to produce high-school graduates who are literate and ready to compete with the workers of any other nation.

WHAT IS BEING DONE?

Many people and organizations have become involved in the literacy issue. Capital Cities/ABC, Inc., and the Public Broadcasting Service (PBS), have national public service campaigns featuring news, public service announcements, public affairs programs, and special local activities on the problem of and solutions to illiteracy. They have organized around a campaign called Project Literacy U.S. (also known as Youth PLUS). Over a hundred organizations—Junior Leagues, the American Federation of Teachers, Kiwanis clubs, and PTAs—are involved with Youth PLUS, which focuses on reducing the amount of illiteracy in our country. The project's sponsors feel that they are having a measurable impact on the illiteracy problems around the country.

- According to a poll commissioned by ABC, 71 percent of the respondents were aware of the illiteracy problem. This was up from 40 percent before PLUS programming premiered. This will be higher in 1989, after more publicity in 1988.
- Calls to the national literacy hotline promoted by the PLUS campaign have increased dramatically. People call the hotline for information that may lead to enrollment in a literacy program. Up from an early average 2,000 calls per month, the hotline peaked at 44,550 calls and now averages almost 20,000 calls per month.

Many famous people, including First Lady Barbara Bush, have spoken in support of literacy programs across the country.

In 1988, a blue-speckled football-shaped object—dubbed the "Readassaurus" egg—hatched a real focus on reading in the American school systems. The Readassaurus egg was "found" April 1, 1988, on Alaska's North Slope. It was flown by the U.S. Postal Service to 20 participating cities, eventually arriving at the Smithsonian Institute in Washington, D.C., on May 2. Unbeknownst to the children who saw the egg and were asked to help it grow by reading books during the summer, twin Readassauruses would hatch from the egg. Schools around the country held contests to name the twins. Eventually, the egg hatched, and the twin Readassauruses, Rex and Rita, encouraged children to read at least three books during the summer of 1988. A little far out, yes, but a very successful program. Children were motivated to read more books.

Ford Motor Co. and the United Auto Workers have sponsored remedial courses at some of Ford's plants because many employees could not be trained on statistical process control, a new requirement in their jobs, because of deficient reading and math skills. Many corporations are joining the campaign against illiteracy, according to "Corporations Take Aim at Illiteracy," an article that appeared in the September 29, 1986, issue of *Fortune* magazine. Some contribute money to community efforts, others solicit volunteers for tutoring the disadvantaged. Dozens of companies, including Ford, GM, Polaroid, Prudential, and R.J. Reynolds, have turned themselves into educators of the last resort, providing the basic instruction that in an ideal world would be found in the schools.

Illiteracy is not a small problem that affects a few percent of the work force. Thousands of workers in every major company appear to need remedial education because of poor basic skills. And, despite the efforts by so many people and organizations, the number of illiterates in the United States is growing. Some estimates claim that the number is rising by more than two million additional individuals each year, in part because of immigration.

IS THERE A POTENTIAL BREAKTHROUGH?

In New York, Chemical Bank, Citibank, the New York Times Company, and J. C. Penney are opening their cafeterias after hours to literacy workshops sponsored by New York's Literacy Volunteers. Almost all such programs, which now operate in every state and major city, are dependent on volunteers who do one-on-one tutoring. It is impressive to see so many volunteers helping people to read, but traditional methods of tutoring are not winning the race against illiteracy.

In the previous chapter, you read about the "Writing to Read" program that was the result of a collaboration between Dr. John Henry Martin and IBM. In 1986, IBM and Martin announced a computer-interactive videodisc program called "Principle of the Alphabet Literacy System" (PALS), designed to improve the reading skills of adults and adolescents who read at or below the fifth-grade level. In the January 1987 issue of *Instruction Delivery Systems*, Atlanta's mayor Andrew Young states that the PALS program offers real hope in the city's battle against social and economic problems. Independent testing has revealed, Young says, that "more than 1,000 of [Atlanta's] 8,000 people in city government . . . cannot read or write." He goes on to say:

> Many of those 1,000 employees are very intelligent and highly motivated people who have worked their way up to supervisory positions. They also succeed in masking their literacy problems, and job-related mistakes—such as misinterpreting water line locations on utility maps—costing Atlanta taxpayers unknown sums.

Mayor Young has made two major decisions to stem his city's literacy problems. First, he installed "Writing to Read" in 83 elementary schools to ensure that the public schools will not create more students who cannot read or write. Second, he gives time off to use the PALS lab to employees who already work for the city.

The PALS course for adult literacy employs many of the techniques used in "Writing to Read." First, it provides people with a failure-free environment, in contrast to the schools they attended, where they were considered failures. Students learn words phonetically, sounding them out before using them in sentences. The students listen to a story about the invention of reading and writing in the mythical kingdom of King Alpha and Queen Bet; the story is presented in colorfully illustrated comic book fashion on a personal computer equipped with a videodisc. Students spend half of each one-hour class working with the videodisc course and the other half using a word-processing program on the personal computer. The intent is to teach students touch-typing and computer skills as well as reading and writing.

The PALS concept was tried out at Cardozo High School in Washington, D.C. where twenty-three students were randomly selected from the bottom 10 percent of the class based on reading skills. According to test results, the students' reading had improved an average of three grade-levels after 20 weeks. Eight of those students went on to college.

The PALS projects substitutes capital for labor. The courseware is based on instructional design techniques. Measurement occurs throughout the learning. The process of learning is motivational. Students who have failed for years in traditional schools are now succeeding. You must visit the sites where PALS is being used and watch the videos that are available to have a full appreciation for the breakthrough that has occurred in teaching people basic skills.

Dr. Martin hired the department of instructional technology at the University of Georgia to be his subcontractor on the PALS project. The program includes over 60,000 lines of code. Once again, it takes a team of subject matter experts, instructional designers, media personnel, and computer authors to create a course that ensures learning to a mastery level. Teachers cannot create such courses in their spare time; It requires central curriculum planning and central course-development work.

After they have been created, the courses can be delivered on a decentralized basis in a cost-effective manner at prisons, in adult learning centers, in job-training centers, and at high schools. PALS labs should be installed on a volume basis in the 1990s to help reduce our country's illiteracy rates. Maybe our prison systems should adopt a practice of not releasing or paroling illiterate inmates. One reason that so many inmates return to prison is their inability to obtain and hold jobs because they cannot read and write. When a state spends $10,000 to $15,000 a year to house an inmate, it can well afford to educate the current population to reduce the growth of prison populations in the United States.

Governor John Ashcroft of Missouri made an interesting statement at the National Literacy Summit held in August 1988. He talked about making "learnfare" part of welfare: "Let's tell the people on welfare that we have a higher view of their capabilities than maybe they do. Then urge them to attend a learning center to obtain basic reading, writing, mathematic, problem solving, teamwork and other job related skills." This may be a key factor in reducing the number of people on welfare. After all, if you cannot read or write, your chances of obtaining a long-term productive job are not great.

Jim Dezell of IBM has summed up the project we must undertake quite plainly: "I think the key point is the application of technology and its ability to deliver more knowledge to a greater number of people in a shorter period of time." Traditional teaching methods will not fix the illiteracy problems of this country. New methods like PALS are essential.

ADDITIONAL HELP FOR CITIZENS WITH LITERACY PROBLEMS

When job-training centers were first implemented in the 1970s by major companies and community-based organizations such as the Urban League, Opportunities Industrial Centers (OIC) and SER Jobs for Progress (SER), there was a large body of potential students who could read and write but who needed word-processing and basic programming skills. Today, those same job-training centers are faced with the problem of students who cannot read and write or do other basic skills such as following instructions.

Some job centers are now teaching English, reading, mathematics, keyboarding, computer literacy, science, social studies, and even humanities through a computer-based training program called the "Comprehensive Competencies Program," or, as most people call it, CCP. CCP began in 1983 when the Remediation and Training Institute obtained support from the Ford Foundation to develop a program that incorporated the best educational practices, approaches and materials for basic skill instruction. The program includes 1,920 competencies in subjects for grades K–12. Once again, students who have failed to learn in the traditional schools appear to be able to learn if they have highly structured motivational course materials, a personal tutor in the form of a personal computer, and a restructured school environment. By 1988, over 300 learning centers in over 40 states and in Canada were using CCP.

With job requirements being enhanced, students not only must be taught with the finest of teaching skills, but they also really need a personal tutoring system with courses developed by instructional designers. As various groups try to restructure schools to raise the quality of learning, it is recommended that they look at some job-training centers, schools inside prisons, Headstart centers, and so on, to see new approaches to the process of education at work. They will see systems similar to the ones that are improving the process of education within employee education. There *is* a systems approach to high-quality education.

A NATIONAL PLAN OF ACTION IS REQUIRED

It will require 12 to 15 years to correct the problems of our primary and secondary schools once a national program of action is developed. Some say it will take 20 years.

The literacy problems could be fixed in four or five years with a national effort by a partnership of business, education, and government. The new administration should make literacy the number one problem to solve in the next term as the nation begins to develop a strategy to improve the overall system of education.

In the last two years, a remarkable movement to overcome illiteracy has spread across the United States, powered by a commitment by and the participation of leaders in all sectors of our society—federal, state, and local governments; business; labor; the media; education; religion; and the nonprofit sector. Everyone wants to help eliminate this problem that is keeping millions of Americans from reaching their full potential as productive citizens. Rarely has a social force emerged with such a wide consensus for mobilizing the human resources of our nation. The goal should be to achieve a fully literate, and consequently productive, America by the year 2000.

13 ///

Applying the Lessons to Higher Education

The worlds of primary/secondary education and higher education are very different. Here are a few of those differences:

- Grades K through 12 have 20 to 30 major subjects, but hundreds of different courses are offered in colleges and universities.
- The school day is very structured in public schools, while the day is very unstructured on the campus. Homework now accounts for a small part of study in grades K through 12, but self-study hours on the campus remain the majority of time spent in learning.
- The college or university is made up of countless titled fiefdoms, and heaven help anybody who meddles with a professor or department concerning what to teach, while K–12 teachers are used to being told the subject, the book, and the course outline.
- Higher education institutions have an amazingly more diverse and complex organization than the public schools. A principal actually manages a grammar school or a high school. University presidents do some management, but they have very little control over professors, deans, and course content.

REPUTATION OF HIGHER EDUCATION

The reputation of higher education today is quite different from the declining reputation of public school education. The land-grant university system is an excellent example of how federal and state governments, working together, can have a major positive impact on education. Some say that the land-grant university system was the single most revolutionary innovation in American higher education, and it happened 125 years ago. Today, more than a million students attend the 72 land-grant universities. Since World War II, these schools have emerged not only as outstanding teaching institutions but also as leaders in research. In addition, our community college system has grown dramatically since World War II. The ability to acquire a college education is one of the great opportunities for American youth.

In its book *College: The Undergraduate Experience in America,* the Carnegie Foundation for the Advancement of Teaching states,

> We have created the world's first system of universal access to higher education. It provides entrance somewhere to virtually all who wish to enroll and offers an almost unlimited choice of subjects to be studied. This system of higher education, with its openness, diversity, and scholarly achievement, is the envy of the world.

When you consider the outstanding private colleges and universities along with the state- and community-supported schools, you see how, in the eyes of the world, the United States has the leading system of higher education. This is in sharp contrast to the current reputation of our public primary and secondary schools, which were once viewed as the finest system in the world but are now looked on as a troubled education system that no longer serves the country's needs.

The reputations of our colleges and universities are so strong that in 1987, 27 Japanese cities were trying to attract branch campuses of American schools. Several schools in Massachusetts, Ohio, Georgia, Maryland, California, and Texas were talking to the various communities in Japan. Even more impressive is the fact that many American professors are teaching in universities around the world.

Most people are aware of how many foreign students are attending American colleges and universities. The best students in over 100 countries apply to the undergraduate and graduate schools in the United States. They often come, according to many students and educators, because the education they seek is tied closely to the high technology that is simply not available outside the United States. They also know that English is the international language of business and science.

Our country has benefited in several ways from this influx of foreign students. First, American colleges and universities normally receive full tuition payments from foreign students because their governments pay the fees. Second, many foreign companies give large grants and research contracts to our universities. Third, many outstanding foreign graduates remain in the United States to work in various companies, hospitals, research centers, and universities.

Over 350,000 foreign students are presently enrolled in our colleges and universities, according to the Institute of International Education. The number has more than doubled since 1970 and has increased sevenfold since 1960. According to the National Research Council, during 1985–1986 a majority of the engineering doctorates awarded in the United States went to foreign students. In the physical sciences, 28.6 percent of doctorates were earned by foreign students. The figure was 19.3 percent in the life sciences. At the elite Massachusetts Institute of Technology, 23 percent of the student body was composed of foreign nationals from 98 different countries. According to National Science Foundation figures, other prominent schools with large enrollments of foreign graduate students (over 20 percent) in the sciences and engineering are the University of California, the University of Michigan, Ohio State University, Cornell University, the University of Chicago, and Harvard.

It is important to remember that today's graduate ·students are tomorrow's faculty, and the trend is definitely in that direction. Many parents are now hearing from their sons and daughters that many of the instructors and teaching assistants in basic courses at our universities are from foreign countries.

Some people are alarmed at how many foreign students are in higher education institutions as well as at how many American graduate degrees are going to foreign students. More surprising is the drop in graduate degrees to American students.

COST IS A MAJOR PROBLEM

The cost of a college degree is one alarm bell that should be listened to, because the rising cost of education is one reason why Americans are not going to graduate school. They look at the cost of two to five more years of education compared to the income offered for entry positions to the top graduates of good schools, and they simply take a job instead.

The cost of a college education and the costs of graduate and professional (e.g., medicine, law) degrees continue to climb each year at a far greater rate than inflation. In fact, the average cost of attending a private university rose 81 percent during the first seven years of the decade! This probably means a 100 percent increase from 1980 to 1990. For public universities, the total cost of tuition, fees, and room and board increased 61 percent from 1980 to 1987. Each family with children in college can tell an alarming story. My father and mother educated their two sons at the University of Illinois in the 1950s for $4,000 each. Not $4,000 a year, but $4,000 for the entire four years. The $4,000 paid for tuition, room, board, books, and fraternity social fees. My sons were each educated for $28,000 at state universities—that is, *seven times* the cost of my own education. My brother is educating my niece and nephew at Princeton and Harvard at a cost of nearly $70,000 for each student, or *seventeen times* the cost of his education! You read stories predicting that the cost of our grandchildren's college education will be $150,000 to $200,000. Your first reaction to these numbers is probably to say, "That is impossible," but the grandparents of our college students today can hardly believe what we are paying. It appears that $200,000 is a realistic forecast unless there are basic changes. Some of this increase is, of course, due to inflation, but not all of it can be charged to inflation. Since 1980, overall college expenses have been rising at twice the rate of inflation.

The cost of a college education and a graduate degree is rising to the level where only parents who have combined annual incomes of $75,000 to $100,000 can afford to pay tuition. More and more parents are asking for financial aid, and most students are requesting huge loans. Students now owe over $10 billion to the federal government for college loans, which is three times the debt of ten years ago. According to one report by the Congressional Joint Economic Committee, a third to half of all undergraduates leave college owing an average of over $7,000. Students at graduate and professional schools often accumulate five-figure debts. Some critics are concerned that these borrowers will be forced to postpone marriage, children, mortgages, and further education. Others are concerned about the educated people in our country starting life with a bad habit of not paying their debts. At the present time, there is a $1 billion default.

Professors and deans are upset that today's students seem interested only in degrees that ensure good starting salaries. What do they expect, given the cost of a college education today? How many students can afford to become social workers in the future? They need the income of an accountant, engineer, or a marketing job to pay off their debts. Young MBAs are flocking to Wall Street to get a return on the investment of over $100,000 that they and their parents spent during six years of higher education.

In the 1950s, a working-class father could, with some real sacrifice, send his children to a local college or state university without financial aid or loans. As we enter the 1990s, this American dream is fading fast. The majority of children of minority and working-class parents will only go to college if the government pays for their education through grants, military programs, or loans. Many people are concerned that the future of higher education will be dependent upon government money for American students and foreign government money for foreign students.

In 1986, then Secretary of Education Bennett called for a college cost-containment program. He said that between 1975 and 1986 average college costs rose 36 percent faster than inflation. He wanted the federal government to limit yearly growth of its student aid for tuition to a rate no greater than inflation plus 1 percent. Needless to say, the higher education community did not react favorably to his comments. The secretary's speech was part of a continuing attack on what he sees as high costs and low quality in higher education, which he said requires "real, profound, and much needed reform." Bennett's comments were an attempt to move public opinion and public policy against increasing college costs, as has been done against rising health-care expenses. He seems to have succeeded in starting some public debate.

QUALITY IS THE SECOND MAJOR ISSUE

On March 3, 1987, *USA Today* devoted an entire editorial page to the message that colleges must cut costs and raise the quality of education. The editorial reported that although we may have conquered inflation during the past six years, college tuitions still increased twice as fast as the cost of living—faster than new houses, health care, energy, food, and cars. As the editorial pointed out, "You don't need a college degree to know something's wrong here." The most shocking assertion was that nobody has any good answers as to why the costs keep climbing. The situation sounds like that of phase 1 of employee education, which is unstructured education with costs out of control. The paper said, "It's time somebody found out," which would, of course, lead to phase 2 (cf. Chapter 10), in which the cost and content of the courses are inventoried and analyzed.

More and more people are asking the question, "Are we spending more on higher education and getting less for our investment?" An article by Peter Brimelow, appearing in the November 30, 1987 issue of *Forbes*, titled "The Untouchables," said that most of America's famous colleges were first founded to train clergymen, and though higher education now trains far more technicians than theologians, it still retains a religious mystique. Educators preach, and parents and politicians faithfully accept the gospel that education is morally good and that more education is morally better. Brimelow went on to raise some penetrating issues.

- We know why medical costs are rising faster than inflation—people are demanding and getting better health care. But why are college costs rising? Are we getting better college training?
- In 1950 the total expenditure on college and universities amounted to less than 1% of the Gross National Product. Since then, it has increased to 2.7% of GNP in 1986, or about $100 billion.
- This impressive growth by the U.S. higher education industry is out of all proportion to what is happening in other advanced countries. Japan ranks tenth in expenditures among countries, with only 0.4% of their GNP spent on higher education. West Germany is eighth at 0.6%. Some people feel that their citizenries are better educated than Americans.

Since 1980, the percentage of college students from families with less than $30,000 income has fallen from 68 percent to 37 percent. If costs continue to rise, the people in this country will be divided into two distinct classes: the rich and educated, and the poor and uneducated. While education is a privilege, it is not one that should be available only to the rich.

The Secretary of Education, parents, and students may be concerned about rising college costs, but the typical college professor doesn't appear to be too concerned. Professors in general feel that education opportunities should be determined by a student's abilities and interests, not financial status. The president of the University of Pennsylvania has said, "We admit students on their academic qualifications, then work with them to find the necessary financial support." This is the typical response from college administrators.

It is not uncommon for a university to have 50 percent or more of its students receiving financial aid. Federal aid is becoming as essential to college students as their textbooks. Some administrators feel that a massive federal program, such as the GI Bill of Rights, will be necessary to fund the rising college education costs. Many people forget that veterans paid for their so-called free college educations by investing two to five years of their lives in wartime military service.

State legislatures and governors have usually supported education because it is not good politics to be against education. However, they are beginning to say enough is enough. The December 1987 issue of the *Illinois Alumni News* said the Illinois General Assembly was not in the higher education funding "mood." The university's president was harshly critical of the legislature's decision not to grant funds. He wrote,

> The action of the General Assembly again points up the fact that Illinois continues to underfund education. The fact remains that Illinois must act promptly to put its fiscal house in order and begin to support its universities and the rest of its education system in a realistic way. Until we do that, the crisis for higher education in this state continues.

Unfortunately, we are threatened with an ongoing annual event called the "crisis in higher education," because administrators want more money every year during a period when there is a stable or declining number of students. They do not want to change the basic education system to be more cost-effective. American colleges and universities could soon be entering a period similar to the great quality decline that has happened in the public school systems. Quality of education is the second major issue that must be addressed at our colleges and universities.

The *Forbes* article cited above contains some interesting facts on quality higher education.

- To broaden their markets, colleges are accepting students who formerly would not have been permitted to graduate from high school. There are colleges where the average student IQ is below 100.
- Department of Education figures show that 87% of colleges offered remedial instruction with 63% reporting an increase in remedial instruction since 1978. The higher education institutions have lowered their standards for students to enter.
- Although it has been little reported, there has been a 20-year decline in average scores on Graduate Record Examinations (GREs) and professional school admission tests.
- There is a heavier reliance on relatively inexpensive part-time faculty, 21.9% of the staff in 1970 and 37% in 1986.

As you watch the decline in quality and hear about further declines being predicted because of cost constraints, you have to wonder if the value of a college degree will deteriorate to that of a high-school diploma.

A 1987 article by Edward Fiske appearing in the *New York Times* reports that American colleges and universities, which have operated for more than three centuries on the premise that the fruits of higher education are self-evident, are facing mounting pressure to prove that their students are being educated. Public institutions in at least half a dozen states, including New Jersey and New York, have begun testing students, first as freshmen and then as seniors, to measure how much they have learned. Assessment of seniors' mastery of their major fields, in some cases by outside professional groups, is also on the increase.

In the summer of 1987, the National Governors' Association issued a report saying,

> Many colleges and universities do not have a systematic way to demonstrate whether student learning is taking place. Rather learning—and especially developing abilities to utilize knowledge—is assumed to take place as long as students take courses, accumulate hours and progress "satisfactorily" toward a degree.

The growing scrutiny is an extension of a nationwide movement that has so far focused on improving primary and high schools. "It was only a matter of time before government officials and other critics would cast their eye on higher education as well," writes Derek Bok, the president of Harvard, in one of his annual reports.

"The trend toward evaluation makes many academics very apprehensive," says Joseph Murphy, the chancellor of the City University of New York. Murphy further states, "A proliferation of standardized testing on the college level would undermine the quality of college teaching because professors will start teaching to the test." Proponents of increased testing dismiss such arguments by saying that assessment techniques have been successfully emplaced by many universities and are commonplace in industry and the military.

Among colleges that are using standardized tests, a popular vehicle is the "College Outcomes Measures Project" of the American College Testing Program. This battery of tests is intended to measure students' ability to solve problems, communicate, and clarify values in social institutions, science and technology, and the arts.

Colorado will require every state college and university to adopt an assessment system by 1990 or forfeit 2 percent of its annual appropriation. Other states are moving in this direction. I predict that university executives will have to implement measurements in order to receive the millions of dollars they request annually. Measurements will eventually become a way of life on the college campus, just as in employee education and the public schools.

University administrators and professors should remember that measurements are not intended just to measure what students know but also to help review course content to see if students are learning the major course lessons. Measurements in education should be a management tool, just as they are in the business world.

A BALANCE BETWEEN TEACHING AND RESEARCH IS REQUIRED

Ernest Boyer, in his *College: The Undergraduate Experience in America,* also claims that

> There is a problem with divided loyalties and competing career concerns within the faculty. Professors are expected to function as scholars, conduct research, and communicate results to colleagues. Promotion and tenure hang on research and publication. But undergraduate education also calls for a commitment to students and effective teaching. Frequently, faculty are torn between these competing obligations.
>
> At many colleges and universities, the priority is clear. A professor who does not publish does not get promoted and never receives tenure. This message places research and publishing as the number one priority. Then teaching is a second priority because the students are waiting for the professor in the class. The students also demand time at the office, which becomes the third priority. The last priority is course development.
>
> The issue seems to be how to create an environment in which research and teaching are mutually respected and equally rewarded. How do we blend these two activities so that a university can maintain excellence in a chosen area of research and also achieve excellence in innovative and quality instruction in the same area? Some schools are evolving to two types of faculty, research and teaching, with new measurements for each.

WHAT SUBJECTS SHOULD BE TAUGHT IS ANOTHER ISSUE

The next big issue facing universities and colleges is choosing what subjects should be taught. Two major issues are being discussed. The first is the amount of remedial courses that are necessary because so many high-school graduates are not qualified to do college work. In a recent College Board survey, 88 percent of all four-year colleges and 95 percent of all two-year colleges in the United States offer remedial courses in reading, writing, and mathematics. Why is this so?

Remember, managing any education institution is like managing an airline. Each seat has potential economic value. Every empty seat is like an empty seat on an airline: It is lost revenue. Therefore, schools will do almost anything to fill the seats. This necessitates providing remedial courses to unqualified students. Colleges and the universities should support more measurements and more programs to increase the quality of public school education, which would eliminate the need to reteach high-school subjects during the freshman year on campus.

The other major issue being debated is the role of liberal arts studies, which have been in major decline for a number of years. The Federal Department of Education has reported that the number of bachelor's degrees awarded in business more than doubled from 1971 to 1984 (114,865 to 230,031) as degrees in English and literature plummeted to 24,419 from 57,026. The shift in student interest from liberal arts to vocational and preprofessional fields over the last 10 to 15 years is well documented.

In a major undergraduate education study made public in 1988, the Carnegie Foundation for the Advancement of Teaching cited "new vocationalism among students." Ernest Boyer, director of the three-year, $1 million research project, writes, "The push toward career-related education dominates the campus, and during the past 15 years it has dramatically increased. . . . At almost all colleges in our study, new vocational majors have been added and old ones have been split up into smaller pieces."

This change is, of course, driven by the job market. The University of Illinois reports that only 19 percent of its humanities students have guaranteed jobs upon graduation, versus 90 percent for business majors. Students also know that universities demand a higher grade average for students entering business and engineering schools. The message is clear: Smarter students—those with a clear-cut purpose in life—will be able to enroll in the schools that offer the most desirable jobs at the end of four years.

As director of education at IBM, I was often invited to many outside education meetings. One meeting was a seminar on making the college graduate with a liberal arts degree more competitive in the job market. I found the meeting a very eye-opening event. First, there were the funny stories told about how uneducated engineers and accountants are. The speakers would say, "You would not believe how many computer science majors couldn't write a coherent paragraph if their life depended upon it." Then there was the famous statement, "With a liberal arts degree, you get an education for life, not just for getting a job." That statement was echoed by almost every speaker. The net message was clear: If you do not have a liberal arts degree, you are not educated, and you are inferior to those who have one.

Of course, in the real world, when you sit in meetings trying to decide where to invest hundreds of millions of dollars in new products or services, you appreciate having the advice of accountants, engineers, and computer scientists, who sound very well-educated. Most of them write well, and they are very articulate at presenting their views on important decisions. Most of them seem educated, whether they have a liberal arts degree or not.

The liberal arts versus vocational education debate will go on forever. Our worldwide competitors are moving in the direction of engineering, finance, computer science, and mathematics degrees. It is doubtful that the dream of more liberal arts courses will be realized unless the bachelor's degree is extended to five years, which will mean a $10,000 to $20,000 additional expense for a college education.

The solution to this debate might cease if the educators in charge of high school and college curricula would sit down and use instructional design techniques for the eight years of education from ninth grade to graduation from college. I predict they would find sufficient time in that eight-year period to teach liberal arts courses, computer literacy courses, science courses, and mathematics courses, as well as the other courses required to get a job. After eight years and $100,000, a college graduate deserves to have a balanced education. The debates over the merits of the 19th-century versus the 21st-century curriculum are really not improving the higher education system. There is a need to apply some form of a systems approach to higher education. If instructional system design methods are saving millions of dollars within employee education, why not use these techniques on college courses to improve quality and contain costs? Instructional design methods and the use of technology are going to have a more meaningful impact on *basic* courses. I am not recommending these solutions for graduate courses, advanced seminars, or selected courses in the humanities.

NEW METHODS OF TEACHING

Changing courses or curriculum in higher education is a great challenge. In 1982, IBM established the Academic Information Systems (ACIS) organization to facilitate the use of computer technology in higher education. Initiatives sponsored by this organization included joint studies, conferences, grants, and over $100 million in donated equipment and funds. The intent was to forge a partnership with professors to develop new teaching methods for college classrooms.

With over $100 million to spend, ACIS was well received by deans and professors. Many professors used their donated personal computers to create courses that were really outstanding. In fact, some people were surprised to find that experienced, tenured professors were more enthusiastic about the program than some of their younger colleagues. The other point of interest was the use of technology in the humanities as well as the hard sciences. ACIS encountered almost no resistance to technology and computers.

Did the learning process at colleges change dramatically because of this major investment in time, equipment, and teaching talent? In the over 3,000 projects there was a fundamental shift in classroom instruction toward more interactive, leading-edge use of tools and away from the traditional lecture method. Professors do not like to be constrained. They believe, of course, in academic freedom, which is important. We do not want to lose individual creativity in the profession of teaching. Many developed or modified the software packages. Each professor used the computers differently. The result was a series of courses that were unique to each professor. All of this happened with equipment from one manufacturer. Add to this effort all the professors who were using other types of personal computers, and you have a great example of diverse and incompatible systems. Several universities are building extensive new networks and developing software to connect all types of computers on campus. By the middle of the 1990s they hope to solve the compatibility problems.

The computer is being used more and more on college campuses but is too often a supplement to "business as usual" teaching methods. Until recently there have been very few breakthroughs in the use of technology to reduce costs.

One such breakthrough came in 1988, when Steven Jobs's NeXT, Inc., (his new company) announced its new state-of-the-art computer for universities. Jobs has the financial support of Ross Perot and the marketing support of IBM. Professors and students will be able to store an unbelievable amount of information and use snazzy graphics to improve their academic work. Many people are predicting that universities will soon have available to them inexpensive computers, which will have the power and advanced functional capability to truly impact the quality of higher education.

Some major companies who give huge sums of money to higher education are not seeing much of a return for their investment. In some situations faculty have reacted negatively. In a recent newspaper article, one professor emeritus wrote that research universities don't merely sell their souls to private industry, they willingly give them away. Some feel that universities should only do basic research. Others on the faculty are very eager to work with major companies on joint research projects because doing so allows them to work on real projects with new money and new equipment.

A trend is beginning in which some large companies are shifting part of their donations to the public school system. In the future, more money will probably flow to those school systems that can quantify the results from a donation. Measurements will eventually be an important factor in education donations. Business executives will begin to expect measurable progress just as they do from employee education in their own companies.

It is interesting to remember that computing was born in the universities and that many developments in computing have been made in the university environment. A great deal of money has been spent by universities on computers. Unfortunately, most university administrators are frustrated by the lack of significant positive effect on the learning process itself. They see islands of outstanding work, but none of it ties together in a system. Too many computers on campuses are used as "hobby shops." The universities need a systems approach to teaching with computers. Setting standards on a college campus is very unpopular, but no organization has achieved major progress with computers until standards are established. Complete flexibility costs millions more than does a reasonable level of standardization.

Professors need to take courses in instructional design techniques and computer-based training. Most faculty members are outstanding subject-matter experts, but they usually do not have the knowledge or experience to do computer-based training. This requires a disciplined approach to ensure high-quality courses. Computer-based training usually requires a team of subject-matter experts, instructional designers, and computer support people. Professors like to develop courses by themselves, not with a team of experts. Only a few universities have set up a central support group to build high-quality courses.

The university environment today is the epitome of unstructured education. If you apply the five-phased approach of Chapter 10, it is in phase 1. There have been many committees, projects, and papers on innovative ideas at universities, but real change has so far been rare. I have been out of school for 35 years, but as I walk around campuses and attend meetings, I do not see many basic changes from the campus I knew in the 1950s.

WHY DO UNIVERSITIES MAKE SO FEW MAJOR CHANGES?

Derek Bok, president of Harvard, in his 1986 book *Higher Learning*, explains why a university does not make major changes. He writes:

> Universities are large, decentralized, informal organizations with little hierarchical authority over teaching and research. These characteristics favor innovation by making it easy for any of a large number of faculty members to experiment in search of better ways of educating students. Unfortunately, the very factors that aid experimentation make it harder for successful initiatives to spread throughout the institution or from one institution to another. Since academic administrators do not have the power to insist that faculties adapt new techniques, new courses, or new curricula, the most promising innovations can easily languish unless some effective force causes them to be emulated widely.

Bok goes on to tell how accreditation organizations are not effective in creating change. In fact, he says, they cause the status quo to be emphasized, because they evaluate a university on standards that have been acceptable in the past. Bok also writes,

> In other walks of life, competition is frequently the mechanism that drives individuals and organizations to surmount such inhibitions and to strive continuously to improve. But competition succeeds only to the extent that customers, judges, or other trusted sources can define success in some legitimate way in order to establish a standard and reward those who best achieve it. In education, at least at the university level, this ability is lacking. Neither students nor other interested audiences can tell how effective their education is or how its quality compares with that of other universities. One reason for this ignorance is a lack of clarity over the ends being pursued. Most professors and students can state in general terms the principal aims of a college or professional school education. But agreement breaks down when one tries to specify exactly which skills, bodies of knowledge or methods of thought are deemed important by the faculty. As a result, students cannot always compare what they are likely to learn at different institutions.
>
> More important than the confusion over goals is the problem of finding out how successful universities are in helping their students attain these ends. On this score, ignorance reigns. No universities attempt to measure the amount their students learn let alone compare the results with those of rival institutions.

POTENTIAL CHANGES IN THE FUTURE

The president of Harvard has done an outstanding job of laying out the issues. On the other hand, the universities are not considering one special form of competition when they say competition will not work in their environment. This is a kind of competition that emerges from an entirely new approach to higher education. Instruction methods and technology exist today to convert up to 30 percent of college courses from classroom lectures to computer-based training. Despite repeated curriculum changes, most universities and colleges still rely on large lecture courses and extensive reading assignments that leave little room for independent thought. These "lectures only" courses could be greatly improved with a combination of a textbook supported by interactive learning on a personal computer.

As an alternative to the way college education is structured today, students could stay at home for one year and earn college credits by taking individualized learning courses that are monitored by a university. The students could earn money during that one year at home to help pay for their years on campus. The new university could provide outstanding interactive learning courses in an advanced technology classroom during the final years of a degree program. If the lessons of Chapters 3 through 10 in this book were applied, the education quality would dramatically increase and the cost of a college degree would dramatically decrease. It is a revolutionary approach, but it is feasible today. Nothing new has to be invented. In the startup years, the new institution based on this scheme might be viewed as an inferior competitor, but this would change rapidly because it would have the measurements to prove that its students learn more lessons than those who attend traditional four-year institutions.

Students might not vote for this new, advanced technology university, but their parents could save $7,000 to $15,000. If the students had to pay the bills, they might enroll in the new university without hesitation. Companies might prefer the graduates of this new institution if they knew that this university had standards and measurements. Even professors might be brought around to teach in such a new institution of education because of the higher salaries it would offer.

Is this idea an impossible dream? The National Technological University exists today, in Fort Collins, Colorado. In this new education approach, students receive lessons from qualified professors at various universities over a satellite classroom system. The students do not leave home, because they have full-time jobs.

A unique but related alternative is the Open University, part of the British higher education system. This institution started in 1971 and now has over 150,000 students a year throughout the UK and has awarded more than 82,000 degrees. Undergraduates have a choice of over 130 courses which are produced by six faculties: arts, mathematics, science, social sciences, technology, and the school of education.

The students are adults who, for whatever reason, could not or did not go on to higher education when they graduated from high school. No significant entrance qualifications are required. Students receive their textbooks and lesson materials through the mail. They tune into radio and television programs on the BBC channels, and they meet their tutors at local learning centers. They now are beginning to use audio and video cassette players as well as personal computers at home for a new level of personal tutoring. The Open University is responsible for course development. They now have continuing adult education courses as well as graduate programs, such as an MBA program and even doctoral programs in certain areas. Teams of knowledgeable course developers devote several weeks or even up to a year to instruction/design and selection of cost-effective delivery systems for each subject.

Another innovative approach could be implemented at a military academy, a graduate school of business, a small liberal arts school, or a school within a large university. This approach would require a very strong leader who could influence the faculty to aim to become one of the finest schools of higher education in the country by implementing the following major actions:

1. Working with the faculty, the school would publish the major lessons to be learned prior to receiving a degree.

2. Measurements would be implemented to ensure that the students learned and retained the major lessons.

3. All students would be required to purchase a personal computer that would be part of the personal tutoring system of the institution. The cost would not be incremental, because tuition would fall because there would be fewer lecture-based courses on campus.

4. The faculty would be trained in instructional design methods to increase the quality of the courses and reduce the length of the time necessary to teach the material. As a result, at least one semester of cost could be eliminated.

5. A computer-support center would be established for faculty use. Faculty would use these computers for developing homework,

exercises, and tests. The school would set standards on personal computers, networks, and mainframe computers to ensure all students and faculty could use the same system. Standards would, also, be established for courseware.

Such an institution would employ fewer part-time faculty, but outstanding professors would not worry about losing their jobs. Their positions would be enhanced because only outstanding professors could teach in an environment in which all students would be well prepared for each class because of the monitoring system that would track student progress.

Schools of education could become examples of excellence by implementing the five key action programs described above. They could practice what they preach. They could become the model for the other professional schools to follow. This restructuring would raise their reputation in the university community from one of the least influential to one of the most important schools. Their resources would, no doubt, increase with their enhanced professional reputation.

If schools of education could influence the quality of education within the larger university environment, they could have a much stronger voice in establishing standards for public schools. They would become the leaders who would develop continuity between expected outcomes for high school education, requirements for college entry, and expected outcomes for a four-year college degree program. This would, of course, eliminate the need for remedial courses in college.

WILL THERE BE MAJOR CHANGES?

Most people in education do not believe any of this will happen. Maybe not, but remember it will only take one outstanding leader working with a faculty that wants to be the envy of its profession to try out one of these plans. I believe some of these new approaches will be tried in the 1990s and that major changes on the college campus will ensue. Some will call this effort to increase quality and contain costs a revolution in higher education.

As business organizations learn how to manage employee education, they will want to work more closely with universities to establish standards for lessons to be learned within a given discipline. Computer science and management information systems departments provide a potential place to begin. In the past, every university has made individual decisions on what to teach in these two related curricula.

"Academic Freedom" has resulted in a great inconsistency in quality. There are outstanding programs and there are terrible programs. Because of this lack of standards, all the major companies have expensive employee training programs that assume students have received only a minimal amount of training during their four years of higher education. What a waste! In the meantime, the number of students is declining in these two important areas of study.

If business and universities could work more closely on the design of curricula and courses, the value of the degree could be enhanced and the cost of employee education reduced. More importantly, students would see how lessons learned in college would be applicable to the job environment. Hopefully, a few computer companies will work with the leading schools of management information systems and computer science to fix this situation. A model of business-education partnership could be established that would work in other areas of the university.

A few educators are concerned that large companies will develop competing colleges, but in today's world of international competition, the large companies have no interest in adding the cost of a university to their products!

Herbert I. London, dean of New York University's Gallatin Division, has written an article entitled "Death of the University," which appeared in the 1987 issue of *The Futurist* magazine. London writes, "I am convinced the university as an institution cannot survive." He is frustrated by lower academic standards and flagging faculty morale. He is angry at diminishing intellectual life, at colleges overburdened with remedial coursework. To accommodate themselves to this situation, he says many colleges have set standards that are roughly equivalent to high-school standards of 30 years ago. London concludes by saying that "what could save the university is some dramatic change, and I don't see that on the horizon."

Let's hope that negative forecasts such as London's are wrong. If leaders of higher education do not want to see a downturn in their current reputation they need to make some major changes. They need a systems approach to higher education.

Senior executives of companies who do not manage education like the other areas of their businesses must live with increased costs and declining quality in education. When they understand that expenses are out of control and that their multimillion-dollar budgets pay for unstructured, low-quality education systems, they implement the lessons described in the second section of this book.

When the senior executives of universities understand the cause for their runaway costs and measure the true level of quality in their institutions, they too will decide to implement many of the lessons learned in other areas of education. Their attitude will change from "Education cannot be managed" to "We must manage education to obtain the required resources."

Higher education is the source of the new employees who fuel the engine of our businesses, government, and not-for-profit organizations. It is critical that colleges and universities produce outstanding graduates. Institutions of higher education must play a major role in meeting the new demand for continuing adult education. They are essential for the technical vitality of our workforce, and many high-tech companies, as well as the government, are depending on these schools for basic research and the production of new knowledge to support advancing technology.

Business and government have given billions of dollars to our colleges and universities over the years. This successful partnership must continue, but the management of our schools is critical to their success in future years. The lessons learned in the restructuring of public education and employee education should be carefully studied by higher education. A greater partnership must be forged between all three major areas of education to gear the work force for success in the worldwide competitive economy.

14 ///

Applying the Lessons to Continuing Adult Education

We are often reminded that we live in a world of change. Some of our parents came from homes that did not have electricity, indoor plumbing, telephones, or a radio. As children they did not have the opportunity to ride in an automobile, fly on a plane, or even use a manual typewriter. They are the people who have witnessed the greatest period of change in history.

Many of us who have worked for 30-plus years remember when organizations thought hard before adding a manual typewriter or an adding machine. Only managers had telephones, and even they had to ask permission to make long-distance calls. There were no copiers and only a few calculators. The few computers that existed had a science-fiction sort of mystique about them. Today, the computer in my house has more storage and computing power than all the computing power that Sears, Roebuck and Co. had up until 1960.

As we enter the final decade of this century, the pace of change has become even more rapid. One change that is coming home to many Americans is diminishing job security. Until the 1980 recession, job security was a fact of life for many Americans. We did not talk about "lifetime jobs" in the same way the Japanese do, but many Americans in fact did have lifetime jobs with the "big companies," which is a term that you hear in Japan. Most of our fathers and grandfathers worked for one company for many years before they retired.

Then came the "downsizing" and merger process of the 1980s. Now, lifetime jobs are very few. Hundreds of thousands of blue- and white-collar jobs have been eliminated, and there is little hope that these jobs will ever exist again. Employees who worked for such well-regarded companies as AT&T, GE, CDC, Honeywell, Kodak, and others known for "lifetime jobs," suffered major reorganizations and layoffs. For many employees, job security has become a fading dream. Some say that the concept of job security is being replaced by the concept of employability. Employability means you must have the right education, training, work experience, and skills to obtain another job when you or your employer decides your current job is not meeting your needs or is no longer required.

In the future, a person will have to think of how he or she can position himself or herself to be a competitive candidate for several jobs. Walt Burdick, the vice president of personnel for IBM, tells new employees and managers that a typical IBM employee will have several major career changes during a long-term career with IBM, which is one of the few companies that continues to practice full employment. Therefore, a person will need to be a competitive candidate for employment and promotion several times during a career, either within one large company or across several organizations. One article has reported that today's college graduates can expect to have seven major job changes during their careers.

THE NEED FOR LIFELONG LEARNING

To stay competitive and employed, an American today must continue to learn every year. There is now a practical, "must do" reason for lifelong learning, whereas a few years ago it was considered a "nice to do." People need to learn more not only about what they are doing in their current jobs, but also about other kinds of work related to their current positions.

Lifelong learning presents a new challenge to our education institutions, business organizations, and government. It is no longer feasible to provide someone with 12 to 16 years of education and then say, "You have been educated, now go to work." Employees are being asked to learn several jobs so that they can work successfully within a team environment. Employees are being asked to train other employees. Being trained and educated is the key to job security in the future.

Many high-school graduates working for manufacturing companies have been told that a high-school diploma is not enough anymore.

Education requirements for technical and clerical jobs have soared. Advancing technology has enriched jobs, but technology means an employee must know more and do more to be successful. More people are being asked to have a two-year associate degree. Employees need more math, problem-solving, statistics, and team-building skills, as well as computer literacy. Junior colleges and technical schools have a great opportunity to fill this need.

Managers and executives are being asked to keep up by attending courses at graduate business schools. The Harvard Graduate School of Business and business schools at the University of Chicago, the University of Virginia, and elsewhere have offered programs for business executives for years. New multimillion-dollar continuing education facilities have been built at the University of Pennsylvania's Wharton School of Business and elsewhere. According to *Bricher's International Guide to Executive Education*, the number of participants in university executive programs grew from 10,000 in 1982 to 14,000 in 1986. The number of business schools offering executive MBA degrees has jumped from about a dozen in 1972 to more than 100 today.

Doctors, lawyers, and accountants are all being asked to enroll in formal programs of continuing education to maintain their professional skills. Professional organizations such as the insurance industry's LOMA (Life Office Management Association) are building courses and programs for experienced workers. Summer vacations remain a popular time for teachers to update their knowledge on teaching techniques as well as on their subject of expertise.

Another major field for lifelong learning will be the in-depth training required for overseas work or work within the international operations of a multinational company. For years, American companies sent managers and executives overseas to their foreign subsidiaries. The local nationals were pleased if the executives learned their language and customs, but really did not expect the Americans to learn them. They made life as easy as possible for the Americans, who often were not the company's outstanding performers.

This is changing. Japanese and European companies are sending their top performers to set up overseas subsidiaries in the United States. They usually learn American customs and the English language. An estimated 10,000 English-speaking Japanese business representatives now live and work in the United States, while fewer than 1,000 American business representatives live in Japan, and only a handful of them speak Japanese. At one time, our technological lead let us set the rules for international business transactions. This is also changing. Americans will have to learn foreign languages and obtain an in-depth knowledge of foreign cultures. The two-day orientation courses of the past are being replaced by eight-month, in-depth preparation programs for international assignments.

Continuing education programs even offer a potential answer to the debate over how much liberal arts training accountants, engineers, and computer scientists should have. The Dartmouth Institute, for example, offers seminars and programs that relate aspects of liberal arts to problems of concern or interest to the business and government communities. The two main purposes of these seminars are to give adult learners a broader and deeper appreciation of the historical and cultural forces that shape their ideas, values, and policies, and to alert them to contemporary cultural trends that may significantly affect the future. Several other well-known institutions of higher learning offer humanities courses to successful executives who must deal with community leaders, lawyers, clergy, bankers, and social workers on broad social and cultural issues and who can therefore benefit from a liberal arts perspective.

Senior citizens are taking an interest in continuing education. "Elderhostel" programs, offering college-level academic courses for senior citizens, are operating across the country. As more and more employers seek to hire retirees, their knowledge and skills may need updating. The Institute for Retired Professionals, part of the New School for Social Research in New York City, opened in 1962. It is the oldest program of its kind in the country and has been fully subscribed since its opening. The institute offers more than 80 courses, ranging from literature to mathematics. Currently, 12 percent of all Americans are 65 years of age or older. In a few decades, the 65-and-over age group will account for more than 20 percent of the nation's population. Many want to work into their 60s and 70s. There is a need to prepare senior citizens for second careers.

LIFELONG LEARNING NEEDS STRUCTURE

So much changes nowadays that providing a "complete education" in high school or college is impossible. Instructors need to teach the basic information that becomes the foundation for lifelong learning. Unfortunately, there is almost no coordination between high schools, universities, and institutions of continuing education. This is a major problem in the education process. High schools and colleges may adjust their curricula to teach "the basics," but there is no guarantee that students will continue to learn as "the basics" change during their lifetime.

I have attended a number of conferences on continuing education. The main theme seems to be that the adult-education mission in the United States is not clear. It consists of an uncoordinated "crazy quilt" of providers caught in the middle of dramatic demographic, social, and technological change. Adult education must change to respond to the changing environment. Partnerships with other education institutions must be created. We must figure out ways to develop a comprehensive strategy for future lifelong learning opportunities. This means eliminating the laissez-faire approach to adult education. The national and state governments need a partnership with education and business to define lifelong learning.

APPLY THE LESSONS LEARNED

The lessons discussed in previous chapters need to be applied to this area of education.

Step 1: Define major careers and jobs

Business and education must work together on step 1. For example, if you are going to have continuing education for retail personnel, the leading retailers should be involved to help define what their employees need to know and do. Education organizations need to know what to teach.

Step 2: Design curricula and courses

Rather than having every community in the country throw together course material to create thousands of redundant courses, we need to centrally develop high-quality courses that include measurements to ensure that the students learn, retain what they learn, and are able to apply the lessons. With so many adults to train, large sums of money could be justified and invested to develop outstanding courses because the cost of development could be spread over tens of thousands of adult students needing the education. The lessons learned in Chapter 5, on quality education, apply to adult education.

Step 3: Use cost-effective delivery systems

Someone has to pay for adult education. Either the government, the employer, or the individual will pay for the education. Why not use technology in education to lower the cost? Technology could also make the education more accessible and more consistent. The lessons learned in Chapter 4, on cost containment, are definitely applicable to lifelong learning.

Step 4: Establish a system to reward learners

Many education institutions today give college credits to adults based on job experience. They are not even testing these adults to determine if they know the major lessons of the course. If an adult can pay a fee, he or she can get college credits, certificates, and degrees. The current system of giving credit for adult education is often a disgrace. No one is suggesting that adults be treated like sixth-graders, but standards must be established. Standard curricula defined in step 1 are essential to providing meaningful education credits to adult students. Adults who work hard in an education system need to be rewarded. Business should be interested in the process of lifelong learning because this could reduce the cost of employee education. Today, adult education courses are rarely considered in job interviews, pay raises, or promotions.

ROLE MODEL FOR LIFELONG LEARNING

Will any state begin this type of an action program? Only time will tell. It is encouraging to read a report such as *Countdown 2000: Michigan's Action Plan for a Competitive Workforce*, which charged a task force to develop a strategy to improve the caliber of Michigan's work force by offering each resident the real oppportunity to maintain and increase quality job skills. The report included statements such as these:

- Establish a professionally staffed public/private policy board to oversee the design and implementation of an integrated, outcome-oriented adult training, education, and supportive services system.
- Develop a standard assessment tool for measuring Michigan's work-readiness goal and definition to use with each participant in all training and educational programs. The assessment will be used to determine incoming skill levels (and thus the appropriate mix of services required), progress toward completion, and in measuring effectiveness of programs.
- A standard skill assessment tool can be used by employers and training services. It can also be used by the policy board as a basis for measuring the effectiveness of programs, issuing annual training service "report

cards" to consumers and "account holders," and ultimately, allocating operating funds and incentive dollars.

- Stop turning people out of the educational system without skills.
- The system must be accountable. We must know what programs achieve, not simply how many people they serve. Programs which receive public suppport must be able to report how far participants have advanced in each of the five skill categories in our new "work readiness" definition of literacy.

  - Language/Communication Skills (the ability to read and write, comprehend and easily use a wide range of printed materials, and speak clearly and effectively).
  - Quantitative Skills (the ability to perform basic mathematical computations, understand charts and graphs, and apply these skills to analyze or synthesize quantitative problems).
  - Problem-Solving Skills (the ability to reason and solve practical problems, follow complex written or oral instructions, and deal with situations in which there may be several variables).
  - Interpersonal/Attitudinal Skills (possession of qualities of self-esteem, motivation, reliability, and punctuality, the ability to deal with and work cooperatively with others, and acceptance of the concepts of lifelong learning, uncertainty and change).
  - Job-Seeking/Self-Advancement Skills (the ability to assess one's ability and ambitions and obtain the skills needed to fulfill them).

- We must know the return we receive on our investments and make future funding decisions accordingly. Programs must become outcome-driven and performance-measured.

Michigan clearly has a vision for a system of continuing adult learning. Michigan's governor, James Blanchard, fully supports the action plan. It may be a role model in the future.

THE NEED FOR A SYSTEMS APPROACH TO EDUCATION

As college enrollment of the traditional 18-to-22-year-old age group dwindles, the number of adults over age 25 enrolling in college on a full-time basis is on the rise. In fact, within a few years, the number of older students may equal that of the "typical" college students. According to the National Center for Education Statistics, the number of older students attending college has been creeping up for many years, from 2.5 million in 1972 to 4.7 million in 1985. By 1991, government officials estimate 5.8 million people over the age of 25 will be enrolled in full- or part-time college programs. This is good news for colleges and universities, which expanded facilities and programs during the last 30 years to accommodate the baby boomers but have recently found fewer students in the traditional age-pool.

The fundamental question to ask about all these millions spent on adult education involves the value received by the individual or the employer. In the past, adult education was viewed as a recreational, part-time, after-hours, even casual endeavor. Continuing education was seen as nontraditional, often low quality, and usually inexpensive.

There will always be a need for the local evening classes at the high school to learn social dancing, how to play bridge, music appreciation, and other "fun" courses. It is not necessary to apply the systems approach to education to these classes. The need to use the systems approach arises when adult education is required to move people to greater levels of knowledge and skill. Engineers and programmers need to maintain technical vitality. Local high school and community college courses are sometimes not enough. Large companies have their own employee education programs to keep their technical professionals on the leading edge. Small and intermediate-size companies do not have these programs. Such programs should exist in institutions of higher learning. Employees should be able to take the courses at home or on the job with computer-based training and video networks.

As new adult learning programs are designed, the following changes in demography, society, and technology need to be considered:

- By 1990, 52 percent of the workforce will be between the ages of 24 and 54.
- By 1995, 60 percent of the labor force will be women.
- 85 percent of workers in the year 2001 are already at work today.

Clearly, adult learners are a large, diverse group who must have education programs to restart, change direction, and move into new fields as well as to provide growth in their existing careers. The needs of this audience demand an education system that is not isolated from other forms of education.

WHO WILL BE RESPONSIBLE FOR THIS EDUCATION?

Millions of adult Americans need to be retrained for new jobs in future years. Who will perform all this adult education? Who will be the lifelong learning leaders? Will there be more structure in the future?

The government is a major factor in job training. The amount of money spent by the government to cope with problems of workers needing training to find new jobs is shocking. In the 1960s the federal government spent $4.4 billion on the Manpower Development and Training Act (MDTA). Billions more were spent by CETA (Comprehensive Employment and Training Act) in the 1970s. If money alone could solve education and training problems, the federal and state governments would have wiped them from the face of the earth years ago.

Most displaced and unemployed workers are not interested in retraining. Crash training programs to solve unemployment problems usually crash themselves after hundreds of millions of dollars are spent. Job-training programs need to be outstanding if the people who were turned off by the education system in their youth are going to be motivated as adult students.

Colleges and universities have a great opportunity to take leadership roles, but this leadership must be earned. When the computer age was already ten years old, no university had yet established a computer science curriculum. In 1960, IBM established a computer science school within employee education and invited university faculty to attend the programs. Some faculty members did, and returned to their campuses to set up computer science programs. In the early 1980s, manufacturing had a low status on engineering campuses. After establishing the Manufacturing Technology Institute, IBM ran a competition to stimulate universities to develop graduate programs in manufacturing engineering and gave $2 million grants to five institutions to support the establishment of graduate programs. Now over 50 such programs are in place. In general, universities are not organized to respond quickly to industry needs. They are weak at tradeoff planning. Their basic response to change is, "Give us money, equipment, and buildings if you want us to create a new curriculum of courses." The world is becoming interdisciplinary, and that is another problem for universities. They have rigid departments, and it is difficult to cut across these departments and disciplines. One reason for this is a lack of a central organization to take action. Talking to a professor or a dean does not mean that a university department goes into action.

As the quality of employee education increases each year, university professors and graduate students are finding it more difficult to meet the new standards. The universities may seem like the logical place to have more leadership and more lifelong learning programs. If this is to happen, however, they need to organize and plan for lifelong learning programs within each major school. A separate college for continuing education may not be sufficient. To be successful, the universities need to apply the management lessons stated in the earlier chapters on employee education.

Education course development companies that are building employee education courses for the large companies will eventually jump into continuing education when they can build a structured delivery system for lifelong learning and can see major revenue and profit opportunities in this area of education. They will probably start with employee development courses. These are the courses that cross department, division, and function organizations. Examples are

- Effective letter-writing
- Effective presentations
- Statistics
- Time management
- Stress management
- Financial concepts for the "nonfinancial" person

Today, these courses are offered in local high schools as well as in large companies. The market is so large that education course development companies will eventually produce computer-based training courses that could eliminate or reduce the cost of many local efforts.

Vocational schools (for both blue- and white-collar workers) can also play a key role in adult education. Vocational education schools can no longer simply play the traditional role of teaching a trade. They want to work with business organizations in developing required courses for industry. Their claim is, "We can do the job better and at a lower cost than most companies because education is our full-time business." Many vocational schools are beginning to use needs analysis, instructional systems design techniques, and technology in the classroom—the methods implemented by the leading-edge employee education practitioners. Vocational schools are more motivated to please business organizations than are many universities. They may play a larger role in lifelong learning than many people realize. Vocational schools see their market as employees who have jobs or who are seeking jobs. Over a million students attend noncollegiate career schools each year. There are 5,000 private vocational schools in the United States, and all are eager to earn a profit.

High school counselors usually have very little information about vocational schools. They spend the vast majority of their time helping students get accepted in colleges and universities. This is unfortunate because many high-school graduates could benefit from vocational schools that prepare them for productive careers as

- Secretaries
- Data-entry operators
- Carpenters
- Electricians
- Welders
- Machinists
- Draftspersons
- Lab technicians
- Chefs
- Auto mechanics

An outstanding example of how successfully a vocational school can provide lifelong learning is provided by the Culinary Institute of America, which the students refer to as "the CIA for cooking." This school was founded (on a very modest scale) after World War II with funds from the GI Bill. Veterans wanted job training, and the CIA was there to take on the huge task of changing army cooks into chefs. Today, the school has a campus on the Hudson River in Hyde Park, New York, and enrolls close to 2,000 students. The program runs for 21 months. The faculty is composed of ninety chefs, bakers, and other instructors. No one tours this school or eats in one of its dining rooms without being impressed. You hear people asking, "Why don't we have schools like this for every major trade and job in the United States?" Some classes start at 3:00 A.M. It is not easy to be a student at the Culinary Institute, but the future chefs take great pride in their work and in their school. The school has recently opened a continuing education division.

Community colleges will continue to be another source of adult learning. Sometimes, these schools have been considered the second-class citizens of higher education, but they are emerging as leaders in delivering customized job training to the companies in their communities. They, of course, give college credits, which are meaningful to those students working toward a degree.

In the future, community learning centers will be established in libraries, high schools, and some profit-oriented centers. Today, no central organization is responsible for adult learning, which means the marketing cost for thousands of community learning centers is too expensive. This will change as more states bring structure and focus to lifelong learning.

Unions, such as the United Auto Workers and the Communication Workers of America, are now working with industry to provide their members with an opportunity to learn subjects and skills that will allow them to maintain employment. The education programs include career counseling and life-planning services. More and more employees are consciously moving toward the view that employer-sponsored training and continuing education programs are a vital part of both work and personal life.

Who will be the leader to bring structure and focus to lifelong learning? Because it is a national issue, the federal government should take the lead. Federal funds are not as important as national leadership. Once again, the emphasis should be on quality and structure so that all this time and expense can truly help people become more competitive candidates for jobs.

It is important that the federal government continue to provide incentives to employers to offer lifelong learning courses and to employees to take the courses. Tuition-refund programs should not be taxed as part of gross income. Employees who work for small companies need to be able to deduct tuition costs so they have the same opportunity as employees of large companies.

A stable, motivated, well-trained work force is critical to the long-term prosperity of business organizations and the proper functioning of government agencies. Companies that provide incentives for lifelong learning are usually concerned about job security. For many, job security in the future will mean being well-trained to do outstanding work. As performance systems measure personal productivity, the value of individuals will grow. We see this every day with professional ballplayers, who are constantly measured on performance. We are beginning to see a similar situation with executives. Executives are paid more today because they are measured more. The outstanding performers are rewarded. In the future, this will be true of managers and workers. Even credit clerks, when they work in a performance-based system, will be recognized and rewarded.

Lifelong learning should reverse the trend toward firing obsolete employees and hiring new employees. If both employers and employees make a commitment to learning and training throughout people's careers, greater job security should result. The value of dedicated, highly motivated, and well-trained employees will increase.

The February 1987 issue of *Training Magazine* carried an article that claimed that the value of experienced and trained employees has been the forgotten factor in the recent merger mania. You can run all the discounted cash flows and proforma statements you want, but it is the employees and managers who meet objectives. Because this is overlooked, up to one-third of all mergers fail within five years. Too many companies are forgetting that change usually requires training. The cost of providing adequate job training to employees after a merger is rarely included in the forecast of merger expenses.

Our country provides security through the public school system up to 18 years of age. With community colleges and state universities, many individuals have a blanket of security until they are 22 years old. Security is offered again when people reach their 60s through Social Security and retirement plans. Now we need to provide the opportunity for lifelong learning to people during their working years, so that they can be productive workers rather than welfare and unemployment-check recipients. Today, lifelong learning receives a minimal effort. Tomorrow, the restructuring of adult learning must be given a maximum effort.

SUMMARY

15 ///

A Time for Vision, Decision, and Action

The fundamental question for education in the 1990s is whether the leaders of government, business, and education will continue to organize task forces and commissions to produce more reports on the problems of education or whether they will take the necessary further step of transferring leadership and resources to restructuring the school systems to make dramatic improvements in the process of education.

To transfer the focus to solutions,

1. The basic process of education is not working in current school systems. We need to reach the level at which a majority of students like school and do well in school.
2. Two basic challenges must be addressed in almost all education areas: how to raise quality and how to contain costs.
3. Based on what has been learned in a few school systems and in the employee education programs of major companies, solutions are available for these problems of quality and the ever-increasing cost of education. *Education systems can be fixed.*
4. The solutions require major restructuring to improve the process of education. Simple cosmetic fixes usually only add to cost, with a minimum and short-lived effect on quality.

221

SCOPE OF THE CHALLENGE

How big is the challenge? The Council on Competitiveness, chaired by John A. Young, chairman of the Hewlett-Packard Company, and including the senior executives of several large companies and unions and the administrators of several large universities, issued a statement in April 1987 that tells the story well and makes it clear what must be done.

> The deep-seated nature of the competitiveness challenge facing America will require some fundamental changes in the way all Americans operate, both in their professional and personal lives. In beginning to address competitiveness, a number of principles should be kept in mind. *First, in developing solutions, America must be bold. A business-as-usual approach will not be adequate to the task that lies ahead.* In addition, competitiveness cannot be viewed in narrow terms. While the trade deficit has been useful in focusing attention on America's competitiveness problems, any decreases in that deficit should not obscure the more fundamental structural problems facing America. Furthermore, recognition must be given to the appropriate roles for the private sector and the government in addressing the competitiveness problem. While public policies create the environment in which firms must compete, the private sector is ultimately responsible for its own performance.
>
> Finally, Americans must overcome their obsession with the short-term and begin to mobilize and sustain the political will necessary to solve the competitiveness problem at its root causes.

Two of the "root causes" of the problem are the decline in the American public school system and the lack of executive attention to employee education and training. Fundamental changes will be required in all areas of education. The solutions must be bold—not business-as-usual. While we do need short-term reform to achieve some short-term results, the root causes are so deep that it will take several years to bring about the necessary and far-reaching changes required.

One major difficulty faced by advocates of systemwide restructuring is that people who work in education tend to view the kinds of organizations in the following list as isolated from each other:

- Day-care centers and nursery schools
- Head Start centers
- Kindergartens

- Elementary schools
- Junior high schools
- Senior high schools
- Two-year community colleges
- Four-year undergraduate colleges/universities
- Graduate schools
- Employee education and training programs
- Continuing/adult education programs

Only the students who are actually going through this series of education organizations view it as an integrated system for education, training, and development. Today, the system is very inefficient. Many subjects are repeated because each education level starts to teach at the lowest point of achievement from the previous level. The leaders in education, business, and government need to work together to maximize the achievements at each level of the education system.

Junior high schools should not accept students who are unqualified to do junior-high work. Senior high schools must demand consistent performance from junior high graduates. Colleges and universities should not permit the high schools to graduate students with higher and higher academic averages and lower and lower academic skills. It is a disturbing fact that the average freshman at a two-year community college can read at only an eighth-grade level, and reports that the average freshman at our best universities has only a ninth-grade reading level are even more alarming. This situation forces universities and the colleges to create remedial reading programs for their freshman classes, as well as remedial writing and math programs.

After paying billions in taxes for various school systems, American companies and their employees are struggling in worldwide markets, and our competitiveness is further damaged by the additional cost of providing remedial training to new employees, the cost of sponsoring job-training programs, the cost of giving money to public schools to reduce the dropout rates, the cost of giving money to schools for various other projects, and the support given to literacy programs. And of course, businesses and their employees pay billions of dollars in taxes to support the criminal justice and welfare system costs that result, in part, from an ineffective school system. In contrast, businesses in other countries are not financing school systems that produce marginally educated graduates.

THE VISION THAT REQUIRES ACTION

No matter what area of education is being discussed, there is a systematic approach to education that will result in high-quality education.

Step 1: Determine what students must know and be able to do at the completion of the education event. This must be done at the detailed teaching-point level.

Step 2: Using instructional design methods, develop high-quality course material that motivates students to want to learn and results in mastery of the lessons.

Step 3: Implement measurements to ensure that students learn, retain, and apply the lessons.

Step 4: Use cost-effective delivery systems that combine high-quality self-study materials with a personal tutoring system that is managed by a qualified teacher.

Step 5: Implement a cost-effective management system within the education organization.

The only limitation to this approach is the requirement that a few thousand students take a course over the life (three to five years is typical) of that course. You do not apply a systematic approach to education when you have a few students in a few classes, but in most areas of education you are dealing with thousands, and sometimes millions, of students who will require a particular course.

As you can see, the process of education does not require a complex solution or massive amounts of research. It is a simple, straightforward process that cries for decisions, action programs, and project leadership. Too many people try to live in a world of complexity. Some educators are like some computer people—they almost worship complexity. The message is rather to keep it simple and get started on restructuring education systems now.

WHO SHOULD BE RESPONSIBLE?

Some organization needs to take charge of the overall education system in the United States. The logical choice appears to be the organization that President Reagan once said should be shut down: the federal Department of Education. To be effective as an agent of change, the department would require major restructuring and some new talent, but all that is possible. Setting up another institution could be wasteful and would put it in the position of competing with the Department of Education.

In today's world, the departments of Labor and Commerce are also involved in education and training. William E. Brock, Secretary of Labor under the Reagan administration, was a leader in championing better employee education and training. Some of the work he did and some staff people from Labor and Commerce could be transferred into the Department of Education. If this were done, the Secretary of Education could become one of the most important members of the cabinet—far more important than what President Jimmy Carter envisioned when he set up the new cabinet post in the late 1970s.

In July 1988, the secretaries of Labor, Education, and Commerce concluded a joint initiative that produced a report entitled *Building A Quality Workforce*. Among the report's major recommendations was to strengthen the education system by

1. Increasing accountability and performance standards
2. Strengthening the content of the curriculum and improving its delivery
3. Recruiting and rewarding good teachers and principals
4. Improving education opportunities for and performance of the disadvantaged
5. Increasing competitiveness within school systems

Ann Mclaughlin, the secretary of labor at that time, took the lead in setting up a commission on work-force quality that will bring together leaders of business, unions, government, and education. A commission such as this, with the partnership of the departments of Labor, Commerce, and Education, may provide an alternative to restructuring the Department of Education. Some government executive must take a strong leadership role to restructure the school systems.

The state superintendents of education and their staffs must become partners with the federal Department of Education to restructure the school systems. Educators must take the leadership role that begins with the federal government and transfer it to the local schools.

MONEY IS NOT THE PRIMARY ISSUE

Based on the lessons learned that are described in this book, there really is no excuse for a poorly performing education system. Instructional designers know how to determine what lessons and skills need to be taught. They know how to develop motivational courses that ensure that students learn and retain the lessons. Personal computers provide proven methods for tutoring students after they hear lessons from master teachers or read the basic facts in a book. The required interactive learning methods are here today.

Business and government should think about results before they throw more money at the problems in education. In a February 1988 *Fortune* article entitled "How to Smarten Up the Schools," the superintendent of schools in Prince George's County, Maryland, is quoted as saying, "Taxpayers are sick and tired of giving across-the-board raises and letting those people who aren't doing the job get more and more money." The article went on to report,

> After all, per-pupil education expenditures between 1950 and 1986, adjusted for inflation, more than tripled to around a breathtaking $4,000, with most of the rise coming in the period when SAT scores plummeted. He believes taxpayers will only tolerate increased spending tied to results such as his planned performance-based bonus or like Rochester, New York's new teacher career ladder. There, as teachers grow in competence through four defined ranks, their pay will go up to a peak of $60,000 for the very best.

Business, which is giving more money to education, may soon start to ask for measurable results. If the public schools continue to be a sinking ship, more and more givers will get off the ship. Most executives are not interested in riding a sinking ship down into the water. They will stay aboard as long as they feel their money and other support can save the vessel. Educators must realize that continuing support from the business community will be based on demonstrated results and improvements.

Business executives are asking more penetrating questions each year about their own employee education programs. They are tired of seeing increasing costs every year for "nice to do" programs. They want a return on their education investment. It is clear that if the process of education is failing in a large business organization, its executives would not try to fix the problem by giving $10,000 grants to each of the company's 300 branch offices scattered around the country. The central education staff would be asked to define the problems, offer solutions, and implement a plan of action to fix the process of education. Looking for solutions from the bottom up is fine if there are minor problems. When the problems are major, the entire process needs to be examined from the top down. Large companies such as IBM, Motorola, and Arthur Andersen & Co. are no longer throwing money at education problems inside their companies. They are investing in education and getting results. No one should expect them to throw money forever at failing education systems outside their companies.

One of the leading schools of instructional design, Florida State University, has done some outstanding course development work in Korea, South America, and Africa. Why so much activity out of the country? Because the ministries of education in those countries admit they need help. They welcome American educators who know how to increase quality and contain costs. These central organizations provide strong leadership to their local school districts.

The two major issues of quality and cost containment were discussed by all the presidential candidates in 1988. The League of Women Voters conducted a poll of their members to find out what topics Americans wanted to hear about from the candidates. Education was the subject out in front. Education beat out health care, arms control, defense, the national budget, and other big issues. Unfortunately, most of the candidates offered only one solution—spend more money. No one was quite sure what role the federal government should have nor how state government should relate to federal and local governments on school issues. Even President Reagan, in his final budget to Congress, proposed a $650 million increase over the current appropriation for the Department of Education with the hope of seeing some improvement in quality. This amount of money could fix most of the problems if properly utilized. Government, business, and education executives should first study the lessons articulated in this book. They need to focus on solutions for improving the quality of education. It is to be hoped that new resources will not be wasted on education in the same way that billions of dollars were poorly utilized during the "War on Poverty" of the 1960s.

I have one great hope: that no more money will be spent on studies. At least 30 major studies and over 300 other studies have already been issued. The studies have defined the problems. There is no need for more finger-pointing. The energies used in the past to create "education bashing" speeches must now be converted to talks about how to fix the problems. Education is a bipartisan issue. The new President, the new Congress, and the new Secretary of Education have a great opportunity to call for new solutions to chronic problems. Governors, the state legislatures and the local school boards all want to be part of fixing education. It is time now for leadership to change education.

WHAT IS THE ROLE OF BUSINESS?

As this book has shown, many people in the business world are trying to improve the quality of education. They all have nothing but good intentions. They have made major contributions in the 1980s by helping the existing school systems. Education is a subject that everyone feels he or she knows something about. After all, every person in any responsible position has had the benefit of primary, secondary, and higher education plus many courses within employee education. The majority of business people engaged in discussing education subjects are general managers (executives), community relations managers, grant-in-aid personnel, and a few government relations people. The vast majority have never been teachers, course developers, managers of education, or had any experience in education technology.

They read the reports and booklets that have been written since 1983, when *A Nation at Risk* sounded the alarm. They even try to compare the reports by taking a subject such as teacher compensation and analyzing all the reports to determine if this is in fact a major issue. They almost never investigate the process of education. Frankly, they do not really realize that the process of education is not working. Unfortunately, most of these business people are not aware of the solutions offered by their own employee education departments because they feel that primary and secondary education is light years away from employee education. Too often, the executive who manages employee education does not fully appreciate how similar the process of education is in all areas of education.

One decision to be made for a greater partnership between business and education is the involvement of executives, education managers, and instructional designers from the world of employee education with the executives of K-12 and higher education. Educators from all areas of education have much to share in the development of real solutions to education's problems.

Where do business leaders fit into this great challenge? First, they need to improve employee education. Too many American workers receive too little or inadequate employee education and training. The lessons of this book should be applied to hundreds of American companies. Executive management should apply the five-phase approach outlined in Chapter 10 to evaluating employee education in their own organization. In most cases, they will be surprised to find out how much money is being spent, not to mention how many courses are "nice to do." They will be shocked at how many of their employees are not receiving the minimal training required for the company to meet its business objectives.

In October 1987, Kenichi Yamamoto, president of Mazda Motor Corporation, ran a full-page ad in the *Wall Street Journal.* It read, "Without the right people, our highly automated $550 million U.S. plant wouldn't be worth a dime." Yamamoto knows the size and scope of his training programs. He knows how much he is spending on employee education. As he puts it, "We believe good people are the key to success. When we invest very large sums to introduce the best in factory design and automation, we also invest in showing our employees how to get the most out of the man-machine equation." At its new plant in Michigan, Mazda has launched what may be the most painstaking recruitment and training programs in automotive history. An intensive five-stage screening process was used to select 3,500 workers from a mass of some 96,500 applicants. Those hired then participated in a rigorous ten-week training course.

Too many American executives do not know the cost of education, nor do they spend even an hour a year to review their training programs. Mr. Yamamoto knows what he must invest in training, and he knows the results he must obtain from his education department to produce high quality automobiles at costs below German, British, and American companies.

Tom Peters, coauthor of *A Passion For Excellence* and *In Search of Excellence,* is telling the executives he consults with to look at their training budgets before looking at their capital budgets. When he starts seminars, Peters stresses that companies must take on bold goals, which include a new focus on employee education and a new budget for "must do" training programs.

The second major area that business executives should continue to support focuses on programs that move unqualified, unemployed, but eligible workers from unemployment to being qualified workers. Unfortunately, millions of Americans have attended school for a number of years without learning enough to hold a minimum-wage job. Job Training Centers embody the type of program that can turn unproductive people into productive workers. Adult literacy programs represent another project that pays real dividends.

There have been predictions of a labor shortage in the United States in the 1990s; in some parts of the country, the shortage has already arrived. In these areas, business must support programs that convert dropouts from the school system to employable citizens.

The third area for business involvement is in continued support for improvements in the existing school systems. Business has done an outstanding job in thousands of partnerships with local school systems. If a company does not have an active program of support for the local school system, it should investigate the opportunities to engage in a partnership with the schools.

The fourth area where business can make a contribution is in helping to define what a high-school graduate must know and be able to do after 12 years in school. Generalizations such as "know the basics" are not sufficient. Organizations such as the Business Roundtable, the National Alliance of Business, and the Committee for Economic Development should invest in research that defines the qualifications the average worker needs. Such research must clearly specify what graduates must know and be able to do. Business should not be the only contributer to this discussion, but its input will carry weight because it ultimately accepts or rejects the graduates through the employment process.

The fifth area requires a special person from the business world. This is the executive who is willing to commit himself or herself fully to helping restructure the public school system to improve the process of education. The key word is *restructure*. This person will have to have the charisma to enlist outstanding people from the government, education, and business communities to design the school building, the network, the personal tutoring system, the logistics, the operating plans, and the management system for a model restructured school that meets the standards and objectives established by the joint business and education partnership. This model restructured school will include new delivery systems. The cost of the future system must be reasonable and justified. There is no point in designing a rich system for rich communities. The cost must be near the average of $4,000 per student per year. The cost of this research on restructuring a school would be a few million dollars over two or three years. Bold decisions would be required. The role of the teacher might need to be redefined. The school day might need to be differently scheduled. There might be fewer administrators. There could be two or three levels of teachers, with some teachers being uncertified. The executive and organizations that lead the effort to restructure schools must go far beyond the current leadership that is setting up the partnerships between business and education in various cities. This is not to say that these partnerships have not made real contributions, but that they just have not explored the basic process of education, which is not working today. Hopefully, this effort will have the support of the new Secretary of Education in Washington.

When this fifth area of work is completed and a delivery system exists, business could contribute the money to develop new courses that could be tested in the new school system. One company could sponsor the curriculum on geography. Another company could support the history courses. Twenty companies could finance the entire course development effort over a five-year period. These companies could be drawn from those companies that today are spending millions trying to help. General Dynamics invested in history videotapes because a survey of high school seniors showed 52 percent could not identify Franklin D. Roosevelt. Others were unable to identify Churchill or Eisenhower. IBM also sends videotapes to schools. The National Geographic Society is spending millions to help geography teachers. All these efforts are well meaning, but until those funds are focused on producing courses that allow students to achieve the objectives set by a renewed school system, the impact of the resources is not being maximized.

The net message is that business should work with government and education to create positive and measurable changes in the school systems. Business should be a demanding partner. Ted Kolderie, a senior fellow at the Hubert H. Humphrey Institute of Public Affairs at the University of Minnesota, writes in the September–October 1987 issue of the *Harvard Business Review* that the best thing business can do for the schools is force them to improve on their own. He says that companies should not hook the schools up to a life-support system of grants and bequests. It is an article that every business leader should read before deciding how his or her company can help the school system. Executives should not give money with only a faint hope that education will improve. In the 1990s, companies should no longer support "hobby shops" that explore technology in education in an undirected way. Business should, instead, start the partnership by making it clear that in the United States we know how to build education systems and courses that allow all students to learn. Black and hispanic students can learn as well as white students. Poor children can learn as well as rich children. Children from broken homes can learn as well as their two-parent counterparts. There is no excuse for an education system that has a high failure or dropout rate. Government, business, and education must share the attitude that they cannot fail to improve the school systems.

WHAT ARE THE ROLES OF EDUCATORS AND SCHOOL BOARDS?

Business should not try to manage the school systems, nor should it finance the public school system. The billions of dollars being spent must be redirected into successful school systems. Local boards of education must be encouraged to look at new methods of learning and new courses. Local boards and school administrators must make the fundamental decisions. Do they want to continue to support old education methods that cost more every year and that result in high failure and dropout rates, or do they want to try new education systems based on new models that can be studied and copied?

As more measurements are implemented in school systems, the value of school administrators will increase. The outstanding superintendents and principals will stand out. They will be paid more as their professional reputation grows. Likewise, master teachers will be recognized and rewarded. Educators should be able to earn outstanding incomes for outstanding performance, like members of any other profession.

Yes, there will be some poor performers, who will feel very uncomfortable. Some of these teachers and administrators are overpaid today. As in any other organization with a good performance and measurement system, the poor performers will be asked to improve or will be encouraged to leave.

WHO WILL SUPPORT RESTRUCTURED SCHOOL SYSTEMS?

Leadership must come from the federal government and the state school offices. Business cannot help to restructure schools without support. Undoubtedly, some school systems will reject all the new ideas. They will defend "business as usual." They will wait for others to try new methods. They will have new and different excuses each year for why their students are not doing well on comparative examinations.

Where will the teachers' unions stand on all these new ideas? Some union leaders will also defend "business as usual." Other union leaders have already recognized that the old approaches are the foundation of a failing system. Albert Shanker is one of the most positive speakers for restructuring schools. The National Education Association is setting up several projects to try to design schools that work. The unions appear to be a stronger force for change and improvement than some writers give them credit for. They want the teachers to work in outstanding school systems.

Parents and other taxpayers will raise some of the strongest voices for change when they realize that new courses with new delivery systems could be installed in existing school buildings and could result in 90 percent of the students achieving A's and B's in basic subjects. Remember, employee education with instructional design methods strives to make everyone a successful student. This is called criterion-referenced training, or teaching to mastery. When employees do poorly, the content of the course and method of instruction are usually the problem. Both can be fixed. The students in grades K through 12 deserve the same process of education.

Parents will also insist that their hard-earned tax dollars be spent on school systems in which their children are turned on, not turned off, by school. Schools exist today in which success breeds success for a majority of the students. When students use the IBM "Writing to Read" program, they show great progress not only in reading and writing but also, to the surprise of many, in math. Teachers tell us that this new learning method causes a profound attitudinal change in children. They gain a positive attitude about school, about learning, and about themselves. The teachers see dramatic improvements in self-image and a dramatic increase in self-esteem, factors which seem to contribute to the dramatic increase in their math scores. One of the most important gifts a school can give a student is success and an increase in self-esteem. The vast majority of American students can be successful, not just the upper 10 or 20 percent of the class. All students can like school, and all can be successful in school.

Another group that will play a major role in this coming revolution is the education course development companies and instructional designers who are now bringing so many major improvements to employee education programs. They will work with publishers and schools of education to create the new courses for the future school systems. They will only apply their talent when new measurements are implemented and new delivery systems are standardized, which is where the business community can make its key contribution to the reformation of schools.

The schools of education will also see the opportunity to help create solutions to the major problems facing our education systems. They could play a significant role by stressing instructional design techniques and measurements throughout the education process. To do this, though, faculty and deans must change their thinking about instructional design techniques, seeing them as good not only for vocational schools, job training, and military training, but also for "pure" education. Any lecture-based course could be improved with instructional design techniques. Professors of education need to work with organizations that use instructional design techniques on a day-to-day basis to see the value. Fortunately, several schools of education have already established instructional design departments. They are moving in the right direction. But many deans of education still need to ask themselves, "Why do successful profit-making organizations use instructional design in their education departments while almost no public school systems use the techniques?" The same question could also be asked of all schools within the universities.

Publishers of schoolbooks will address the crisis in a variety of ways. Some will defend "business as usual" until they sell their last book. After all, their system has been in place for over a hundred years, and the textbook business is huge. Other publishers have already seen the value of new course development and teaching methods. Some publishers have merged with or purchased education course development companies that employ instructional designers. Too often, the mergers have not been perfect matches because the publishers tend to let subject-matter experts write books and develop courses rather than teaming up the subject matter experts with instructional designers. Outstanding course materials, including textbooks, will always be required in the process of education.

If major business organizations step forward with funds to create new courses for the restructured school systems, the publishers and the graduate schools of education will probably be asked to build the new courses. Remember, the new contracts for building courses will have a set of objectives and measurements that require students to master the information. Publishers and schools of education will be required to be A performers in course design. If they are not, the contracts will go to the education course development companies that are already working successfully with employee education departments in government agencies and large corporations. Once the measurement system and the delivery systems are in place, these companies know how to build successful courses.

THE TIME FOR LEADERSHIP

All this change will test the leadership of our country. It is clear that American education systems cannot undergo major reform in their basic structure unless this reform is undertaken by a strong partnership between government, business, and education. No one group can do it alone. The cost of fixing the education systems is reasonable. The incremental cost is in the millions, not billions. Tradeoff planning will be necessary. The resources being spent today must be redirected from unsuccessful courses and learning methods to successful new education systems. An expensive, successful education system should not be built on top of an expensive, failing system.

The leadership will require, as always, a few people with vision who are capable of describing a clear picture of where we must go to have a successful education system. They must be able to take the verbal abuse that will be thrown at them by thousands of "education experts" who will say, "You cannot change the system. It may not be a perfect system, but this is how education is done. It is different from business and government. Measurements and performance systems cannot work." Education is the last major industry that says that technology is not affordable and that refuses to work under central direction.

The leaders of change will be people who have managed major changes in other areas as well as those education leaders who have been advocating change for a number of years. They must have a consuming sense of purpose. Long-term commitment will be necessary. They must be able to deal persuasively with people who can help their programs and with those who can hinder their programs. They must be able to cut through nonessentials and weak excuses to reach the important decisions essential for change. The people who manage change must not only have a vision, they must be able to sell the vision and, most importantly, to implement the vision. The United States was built on this type of leadership. Our ability to create and manage change is the marvel of the world.

The American education system was one of the key factors in the success of the United States during the past century. There is no doubt that the American education system can be changed and reformed. The American education system can evolve from an attendance-based system to a performance-based system that insures measurable results. Our system can be transformed into the envy of the world again. The know-how exists in this country. Right now, leadership is the only missing part of the success formula. The resources to do the job exist. The leadership for the revolution in education will emerge in the 1990s.

Quality was the big issue in the 1980s. Education will be the big issue in the 1990s. Our country reached the moon by the end of the 1960s when that goal was set by the President of the United States early in the decade. Hopefully, our new President will set a similarly high goal for education in the 1990s.

We need to raise education to a national priority. The education of our citizens, our workers, and our children is the most important element for success in the next century. We need to take the lessons that have been learned in the 1980s and apply our best thinking to the second round of education reform. The United States needs to have the finest workforce in the world to compete in the global market. Having the world's finest education system is not a "nice to do," it is essential if we are to maintain our current standard of living.

Americans do not want two groups of citizens—one group composed of educated people with good-paying jobs and the other of dropouts who spend their lives on government support. The second group is growing every day. The productive citizens will soon realize that much of their work is for taxes to pay for the second group, who cannot or will not work.

Lester Thurow, the dean of the Sloan School of Management at the Massachusetts Institute of Technology has said, "If America is to regain a competitive edge, it will have to develop the less educated half of the workforce, because a trained workforce—unlike money, managers, and technology—is the only ingredient for economic development that cannot be easily moved almost anywhere in the world."

Business executives, government leaders, and educators have been saying for years that "people are our most important asset." With new methods of learning, a new systems approach to course development, and new cost-effective delivery systems, all the leaders in our country have an opportunity to unite behind a new national priority, which is the revitalization of the entire education system in the United States. We can hope that this moment of opportunity will not be lost because of a lack of leadership.

References

Introduction

Carnegie Founation for the Advancement of Teaching. *An Imperiled Generation: Saving Urban Schools.* Princeton, N.J.: Carnegie Foundation for the Advancement of Teaching, 1988.

"Schools Report: Nation Still at Risk." *Norwalk Hour,* April 25, 1988.

U.S. Department of Education, National Commission on Excellence in Education. *A Nation at Risk: The Imperative for Education Reform,* Washington: Government Printing Office, 1983.

Chapter 1

Brimelow, Peter. "Are We Spending Too Much on Education?" *Forbes,* December 29, 1986, 72–76.

Simon, Paul. *Let's Put America Back to Work.* Chicago: Bonus Books, 1987.

"Still a Nation at Risk?" *Norwalk Hour,* February 19, 1987.

Tucker, Marc S. *A Nation Prepared: Teachers for the 21st Century.* Rochester, N.Y.: National Center for Education and the Economy, 1986.

U.S. Department of Education. *Japanese Education Today.* Washington: Government Printing Office, 1987.

Chapter 2

American Society for Training and Development. *Serving the New Corporation,* 1986.

Chmura, Thomas J., Douglas C. Henton, and John G. Melville. *Corporate Education and Training.* Stamford Research Institute Reports, no. 753. Stamford, Conn.: Stamford Research Institute International, 1987.

Chapter 3

Chmura, Thomas J., Douglas C. Henton, and John G. Melville. *Corporate Education and Training.* Stamford Research Institute Reports, no. 753. Stamford, Conn.: Stamford Research Institute International, 1987.

"Express Training." *P.C. World.* November, 1987.

Chapter 10

Tichy, Noel, and Mary Anne Devanna. *The Transformational Leader.* New York: John Wiley & Sons, 1986.

Chapter 11

Committee for Economic Development. *Investing in Our Children: Business and the Public Schools.* 1985.

"Dodd Calls for Computer Education." *Norwalk Hour,* August 11, 1987.

Kearns, David T., and Denis P. Doyle. *Winning the Brain Race: A Bold Plan to Make our Schools Competitive.* Institute for Contemporary Studies Press, 1988.

Levine, Marrsha, and Robert Trachtman. *American Business and the Public School: Case Studies of Corporate Involvement in Public Education.* Committee for Economic Development, 1988.
Otto, Kenneth L. *Attitudes Toward Primary and Secondary Education Systems.* Business Roundtable, 1986.
"Teachers Block Education Reform." *Norwalk Hour,* April 6, 1987.
U.S. Department of Education. National Commission on Excellence in Education. *A Nation at Risk: The Imperative for Education Reform.* Washington: Government Printing Office, 1983.
U.S. Department of Education. *Japanese Education Today.* Washington: Government Printing Office, 1987.
"Why School Reform Isn't Working." *Fortune,* February 17, 1986.

Chapter 12

"Corporations Take Aim at Illiteracy." *Fortune.* September 29, 1986.
Hudson Institute, Inc. *Workforce 2000: Work and Workers for the 21st Century.* 1987.
Jennings, Peter (reporter). *At a Loss for Words: Illiterate in America.* American Broadcasting Corporation (broadcast), September 3, 1986.
"Martin, IBM Team Up Again." *Instruction Delivery Systems.* January-February, 1987.
National Alliance of Business. *Atlanta 2000: Adult Illiteracy and the Consequences,* 1988.
U.S. Departments of Labor and Education. *The Bottom Line: Basic Skills in the Workplace.* Washington: Government Printing Office, 1988.

Chapter 13

Bok, Derek. *Higher Learning.* Cambridge: Harvard University Press, 1986.
Boyer, Ernest. *College: The Undergraduate Experience in America.* Princeton, N.J.: Carnegie Foundation for the Advancement of Teaching, 1986.
Brimelow, Peter. "The Untouchables," *Forbes,* November 30, 1987.
"Colleges Prodded to Prove Worth." *New York Times,* January 18, 1987.
"Cross Winds Buffet Land-Grant Colleges as States' Needs Shift." *Wall Street Journal,* March 31, 1987.
London, Herbert I. "Death of a University." *The Futurist,* April 1987.
"Reagan Official Urges Cap on Aid for College Tuition." *Wall Street Journal,* November 20, 1988.
University of Illinois. *Alumni News,* December 1987.

Chapter 14

Geber, Beverly. "The Forgotten Factor in Merger Mania." *Training Magazine,* February, 1987.
Michigan. Governor's Cabinet Council on Human Investment. Adult Literacy Task Force. *Countdown 2000: Michigan's Action Plan for a Competitive Workforce.* Lansing, Mich.: 1988.

Chapter 15

Council on Competitiveness. *Confronting the New Reality.* 1987.
Kolerie, Ted. "Education That Works: The Right Role for Business." *Harvard Business Review,* September-October, 1987.
Magnet, Myron. "How to Smarten Up the Schools." *Fortune,* February, 1988.
"Tom Peters on Excellence." *San Jose Mercury News,* October 1, 1987.
Thurow, Lester Carl. "Address in the David Kinely Lecture Series." Champaign, Ill.: University of Illinois Business School Publications, 1988.
U.S. Secretaries of Labor, Education and Commerce. *Building a Quality Workforce.* Washington: Government Printing Office, 1988.

Index